BLESSING & HONOR HONOR & BLESSING

Understanding The Confusion/Deception of Biblical Spin

23 March 2000

To Pastor Paul Taylor - Dawn -

[illegible signature]

Isaiah 40:8

BLESSING & HONOR HONOR & BLESSING

Understanding The Confusion/Deception of Biblical Spin

Captain John H. Kaelberer
CHC, USN, Ret.

WINEPRESS WP PUBLISHING

Printed in the United States of America

Packaged by WinePress Publishing, PO Box 428, Enumclaw, WA 98022. The views expressed or implied in this work do not necessarily reflect those of WinePress Publishing. Ultimate design, content, and editorial accuracy of this work is the responsibility of the author(s).

ISBN 1-57921-261-1
Library of Congress Catalog Card Number: 99-67818

DEDICATED TO

The Rev. Dr. Robert David Preus

Confessional Lutheran Theologian—Man of God

In 1953, Robert D. Preus preached a sermon at the centennial convention of the Norwegian Synod. It came to be known as the "Our Mission As A Remnant" sermon. In that sermon can be seen his commitment to God's inerrant and infallible Word, a commitment that was the center of his teaching and preaching. His students will always remember his love for God's Word and for the Lutheran Confessions, which are expositions of that Word. In that sermon he proclaimed:

> The church of God must be content to remain a struggling, militant minority. Thus it has always been and always will be. God will have it no other way. . . . Remember, our rightness or wrongness, our success or failure, will never be measured by counting noses, but by something which will stand forever and will judge men in the last day, the Word of God.

From Robert David Preus, In Memoriam, 1924–1995, in LOGIA, vol. V, (Epiphany 1996) No.1, p.3.

About the Author

John (Jack) Herbert Kaelberer was born on 2 October 1929 in Philadelphia, Pennsylvania, to Emma and Herbert Kaelberer. He is a graduate of Muhlenberg College, Allentown, Pennsylvania, and the Lutheran Theological Seminary at Philadelphia, Pennsylvania. He was ordained by the United Lutheran Church in America on 20 May 1954. He also holds masters degrees from the Lutheran Theological Seminary at Philadelphia in divinity and from the United States International University, San Diego, California, in human behavior.

He served St. Paul's Lutheran Church, Allentown, from 1954 to 1956 and St. John's Lutheran Church, Hatboro, Pennsylvania from 1956 to1965. He entered active duty in the Chaplain Corps, United States Navy, in 1965 and retired from active duty in the rank of Captain on 1 September 1989.

Among his many assignments were:

- Destroyer Division 212; Naval Hospital, Oakland, California
- 1st Marine Division (FMF), Vietnam
- Naval Station, San Diego
- USS Chicago (CG-11)
- Naval Postgraduate School, Monterey, California
- Office of the Chief of Chaplains, Washington, D.C.
- Force Chaplain, Fleet Marine Force, Pacific, Hawaii
- Command Chaplain, Marine Corps Recruit Depot, San Diego
- Fleet Chaplain, U.S. Atlantic Fleet, Norfolk, Virginia.

Among his awards are:

The Legion of Merit Medal, The Bronze Star Medal with Combat V, The Meritorious Service Medal, The Navy Commendation Medal, The Vietnam Cross of Gallantry, Various Vietnam campaign ribbons.

In 1985, Chaplain Kaelberer entered the ministerium of the Lutheran Church-Missouri Synod, after twenty-nine years of serving the United Lutheran Church in America, which became the Lutheran Church in America. He is married to the former Barbara Gay Moyer of Bloomsburg, Pennsylvania. They have three children: John H. Jr., Rev. Eric V., and Mrs. Mary Joan Moulton.

Acknowledgments

I gratefully acknowledge the encouragement of family and friends who challenged me to write this book. Warren Rangnow, a special friend from the days of my youth, headed the cheering section. I offer my thanks to the Rev. Jeffrey Pulse, my pastor, and the Rev. Richard Andrus, both of Bremerton, Washington, for their counsel and kindness in reviewing sections of this work. Special thanks are extended to my son, the Rev. Eric V. Kaelberer, for his wise comments and for writing the foreword. My wife, Barbe, has been my right arm in editing and proofreading this manuscript. Above all, my greatest appreciation is for her love and for her prayers that this work might be to God's glory and for God's people that they may enjoy forever the honor and blessing of God's Word, His love message in Jesus.

Foreword

Dear Reader,

It is my pleasure to introduce you to a work that is long overdue. You, the lay person, whether within or outside the Christian church, may not be aware of the attack by some theologians and philosophers upon the Word of God; an attack which uses deception and confusion. It is important to become aware of what has happened, and is happening today, in regard to the interpretation of Holy Scripture, God's love message in Jesus to you. As this work unfolds, this deception and confusion will be revealed so that God's Word in all its purity and power may honor and bless you in Jesus Christ, Who is the center and Truth of all Scripture.

The author is my father. He has served both as a parish pastor and in the service of his country as a U.S. Navy chaplain. His ministry and life as a chaplain/pastor is woven throughout the pages of this work. Often, in works on theology, the author is downplayed so that the subject matter may be brought to the forefront. In this book, the tapestry, which is my father's life, his autobiography, is woven into the theological presentation. Why, you may ask? Because theology never happens in a vacuum. The God of the cradle and the cross, came for people. He lived as we live. Lives matter to Him.

In this regard, you will find this book honors you. Often the professional theologian refers to you, or you refer to yourselves, as "just a layman," or "simply a lay person." What comes through in the pages of this book is something that I learned from childhood at my father's knee: There is no such thing as "simply a lay person." From Scripture, Dad taught me how God honors us, how He honors you. As he taught me, so he seeks to instruct you with this simple, biblical truth: You are the object of God's love. You are worthy of His attention and concern, even as the Cross and the Empty Tomb prove.

With fondness I remember when my father, then a chaplain who had experienced the realities of life and death in the Vietnam War, asked for an assignment in post-graduate study. These were times when such assignments were hard-won. Many would-be students wrote long essays on why they should be selected. Entering my dad's study one day, I saw him finishing his application for graduate study in human behavior. His letter of rationale for study in one sentence stated: "I desire to study man, the object of God's love in Jesus Christ." That short sentence has resonated in my life ever since. By the way, he was accepted for post-graduate study.

This is also his reason for writing this book for you. He sees you as the object of God's love in Jesus Christ. "Just a lay person?" No, you are God's beloved son or daughter. In the pages that follow, you will read, and I pray be disturbed by, the modern theological trends which seek to focus your attention and the church's attention, anywhere and everywhere, except on the God who has revealed Himself in the Holy Scriptures.

Dad's title and thesis, "Blessing & Honor / Honor & Blessing," is an autobiographical journey through the inner sanctum of theology and life. In our day, when theology and life are pried apart (kept separate), this work gives them the honor they deserve. He brings them together, showing that the God of Holy Scripture is the God who is also "the God for you."

From this perspective, you will see that God's blessing and His honor are tied together. Where He is blessed, there His honor shines forth brightly. Where He is honored, there His blessing will be found.

Such blessing and such honor are founded, grounded, and rooted in the Word of God. This is central, not only to this work, but also to life itself.

Some time ago, having finished reading a draft of this book, my father asked me about a reference work to which you, the reader, could be directed for further study. Reading this book again, I can think of only one reference, and it is the "one true" reference to which this book dispenses all its blessings and from which it gives all honor, the Holy Bible, the Word of God. It is the only reference to which this book and its human author directs you. There you will indeed find blessing and honor, honor and blessing.

With thanks to God for the honor of writing this foreword, I am, most proudly, the author's son.

Pastor Eric V. Kaelberer

Contents

INTRODUCTION

This book is written to the glory of God and in honor of His powerful Word in Holy Scripture. It is written for you, who may be confused concerning how God's Word has been interpreted to you in recent years. God's Word in Scripture has taken quite a beating, not from enemies of Christ, but from those who have been and are theologians within the Christian church. Philosophers have crept in to add their theories, and they have also muddied the lucid clarity of Holy Scripture. What unfolds within these pages is an explanation of the attack and the judgment of biblical scholars, as well as philosophers, on the inerrancy and infallibility of God's Word in Scripture.

The late Dr. Robert D. Preus, former President of Concordia Theological Seminary, Fort Wayne, Indiana, to whom this book is dedicated, was the first person to welcome me as a pastor to the Lutheran Church-Missouri Synod (LCMS). In 1984, I was a senior Navy Captain chaplain on active duty representing the Lutheran Church in America (LCA), which later merged with the American Lutheran Church (ALC) and the Association of Evangelical Lutheran Churches (AELC), becoming the Evangelical Lutheran Church in America (ELCA). Later, I will tell how and why the Lord led me away from the LCA to the LCMS. The "how" and the "why" are woven into the title of this book: *Blessing & Honor / Honor & Blessing.*

Even before my colloquy process (the means by which clergy of other church bodies are certified for admission to the clergy roll of the LCMS) was completed in the summer of 1984, Dr. Preus and I had a meeting in his Fort Wayne office where we shared what God's Word meant to us. That afternoon will always be emblazoned upon my heart and mind as we were one, not only in prayer, but in our love for Jesus as the Living Word and for His Holy Scriptures as the written Word of God. For years I had longed for such a biblical and theological relationship from my church.

Dr. Preus embodied in spirit and person the reality, the sum and substance, of what a confessional theologian is: a biblical scholar who believes in God's Word in Holy Scripture as the norm and absolute standard for all Christian doctrine. Dr. Preus regarded all of Scripture as God's inerrant and infallible message to man. As we shook hands and parted, his words "Welcome, Jack!" came to my ears. I knew I was home in the Lutheran Church I knew as a child. Our time together was unhurried and free, a time that I will cherish forever. On 4 November 1995, God called His faithful servant to Himself.

If, per chance, you have a "good handle" on the Word of God in Scripture and have been unaffected by the confusing ideas and theories that have surfaced in recent years, and even in the years since the Enlightenment, this book may not be for you. However, I suspect from the contacts I have had as a chaplain/pastor that you have questions about the way the Holy Scriptures have been presented to you. There may be within you a spiritual hunger, a deep longing for an understanding of what has happened to God's Word in Scripture, the Scripture that was so plainly presented to you in your youth. You may be in a church where Scripture is honored as the infallible and inerrant Word of God. As such, you are blessed beyond measure but may be interested in understanding what has transpired over recent centuries in which God's Word has been held in question. If so, read on.

As a Navy chaplain and a parish pastor, I have seen spiritual hunger firsthand on the battlefield as well as in the parish setting. In both settings, in war or in peace, the pastor or the chaplain has to ask the following questions based upon his theological orientation of the Word of God: How do I faithfully feed the people of God? Do I feed them the Word of God as that Word is proclaimed in Scripture; or do I bend, copy, and parrot theories my theological education influences me to preach and teach, wherein all sorts of questions surface regarding the Word of God in Scripture? Is the Bible the Word of God? Do I attack it, or dismiss it? Do I throw to them the husks of man's ruminations in theological thought which are based on man's superiority of thought over and against that which God has decreed in His Holy Word?

Sadly, anything short of preaching God's Word as His inerrant and infallible word represents the *greased pig* of pulpit proclamation. When pastors and chaplains waffle and hedge concerning Holy Scripture being the Word of God in every respect, God's people have been deceived. The "greased pig" of pulpit proclamation comes encased in uncertainty, confusion, and deception, because it is not grounded in that which God has revealed in Holy Scripture as His Word. It is proclamation from a source foreign to Scripture, a proclamation that does not honor God or bless

His people. Its slipperiness leaves nothing for God's people to hold onto with certainty as coming from God. Pulpit proclamation apart from the truth of God's inerrant and infallible Word can only be man's intrusion of fallible thought upon the people of God.

In churches where Scripture is not honored and declared as the Word of God, new authorities and emphases emerge. Scriptural doctrines, faithfully held by Christians of ages past, are discarded or questioned into oblivion. New twists to doctrine and to God's Word come as newfound authority, which "pulpiteers" seize with delight as fresh revelation from heaven. Liberal doctrine now takes on the character of the stock market—up and down. Words like *justice, pluralism, diversity, liberation, process,* and *feminism* bounce off nave walls. God is referred to as *She* or *Sophia*—words the laity never heard coming from pulpits twenty years ago. You ask, "What is truth? What is going on in my church? Who and what am I to believe?" Does this mean God has steered so far off course that what was once clear and lucid, now needs a course correction? Confusion reigns. Does this mean God has lost, and His future is in doubt, and the prince of darkness has won?

The influence of theologians and philosophers, past and present, upon orthodox Christian theology is disastrous. Their influence will be seen in following chapters. This book is written so that you can understand and be forewarned concerning present or future deception that has been or might be laid upon you. At stake is the spiritual life of family, church, community, nation, and world. This book is a broad overview of the confusion and deception and is not intended to rise to the level of a theological seminary course. It is written so that God's Word may be seen as His inerrant and infallible message in Jesus, from Genesis to Revelation.

Over 2300 years ago, a Chinese writer by the name of Sun Tzu wrote a military classic entitled, *The Art of War.*

Contained therein are principles for the conduct of war. In his first chapter, point seventeen for the plans of war states, "All warfare is based on deception"[1] Sun Tzu lived from 400 to 320 BC.

As a Navy chaplain who served with the 11th Marine Regiment of the First Marine Division in Vietnam from July 1969 to July 1970 and from 1965 to 1967 with two deployments to the waters off Vietnam with the United States Navy, I can echo the strategy of that Chinese writer that deception is the tactic of waging war. In order to confuse the enemy, I recall how on the wardroom table of the USS STODDARD (DD-566), we would roll dice to determine our next approach to bombard North Vietnamese shore gun emplacements, which were protecting the coastal flow by sampans of arms and munitions to the Viet Cong and the North Vietnamese Army (NVA). The deception of the "roll of the dice" was a tactic of war.

Deception is confusion. This has been the basic warfare tactic of the prince of darkness long before Sun Tzu applied the tactic to successful military warfare. Could it be that Sun Tzu learned it from him? We see its first use in Genesis 3:1–5:

> Now the serpent was more crafty than any beast of the field which the Lord God had made. And he said to the woman, "Indeed, has God said, 'You shall not eat from any tree of the garden'?" And the woman said to the serpent, "From the fruit of the trees of the garden we may eat; but from the fruit of the tree which is in the middle of the garden, God has said, 'You shall not eat from it or touch, lest you die.'" And the serpent said to the woman, "You surely shall not die! For God knows that in the day you eat from it your eyes will be opened, and you will be like God, knowing good and evil."

This is deception based upon confusion. Two voices speak with authority—God, the Creator, and the serpent. Which voice is to be obeyed?

This question of obedience to God's authority is still the major spiritual issue of our day. Many voices today come to your hearts and ears. They come with deceiving, confusing authority, with one exception, and that one exception is the voice of God in His Holy Word.

This book deals with a theological subject called *hermeneutics*, which is the study of the methodological principles of interpretation of the Bible. In Chapter 1, I will further explain this high and mighty word, *hermeneutics*, a word that too often is consigned to seminary classrooms and not to the every day life of the people of God. In truth, it should be and must be understood for spiritual life to grow and thrive.

Notes

1. Sun Tzu, *The Art Of War,* trans. Samuel B. Griffen, (London: Oxford University Press, 1964), 66.

Chapter 1

Hermeneutics

Thy word is a lamp to my feet, And a light to my path.
(Ps. 119: 105)

Wow! That word *hermeneutics* sounds like a physical disorder much like lupus erythematous. The latter refers to a physical disorder characterized by skin inflammation. The former refers to the interpretation of Holy Scripture as all literature is open to interpretation, whether a fictional novel or a do-it-yourself manual on home construction.

The word *hermeneutic* comes from the Greek word, *hermeneuein,* used with variations to mean "translate," "explain," and "interpret." It tries to shrink or diminish the distance between the writer of Scripture, and you and me, the readers.

It is also thought that the Greek word can be associated with the name of the Greek god Hermes, who in mythology is identified as the son of Zeus and Maia, who was the messenger, or herald, of the gods, and thus was in the communication business. The Romans turned Hermes into their god named Mercury. The floral business has adopted the image of Mercury with his winged feet as their logo for FTD (Floral Transworld Delivery).

Hermeneutics may be a strange and unfamiliar word to you. My wife and I live in Port Ludlow, Washington, an area populated by retired business and professional people who have church affiliations to a greater degree than we found in our former community, La Mesa, in sunny, southern California. However, when I shared with them that I was in the process of writing a book about hermeneutics for the lay person, they would raise their eyebrows and ask, "What is hermeneutics?" Once I told them that hermeneutics, especially biblical hermeneutics, is concerned with the interpretation of Holy Scripture, they understood.

Hermeneutics. Is this a word to be consigned to seminarians and the clergy as one of their exclusive areas of study? Indeed, is it a word-shield to keep the common folk of the pew from invading the sanctity of the proclamation from the pulpit, so that they do not question the preacher, the keeper of hermeneutics, the keeper of the key to biblical interpretation?

The truth is that you are caught up in the implications of this word, *hermeneutics*, whether or not you choose to be involved. The involvement is inescapable, because hermeneutics is about the Christian faith, both positive, as well as negative. It is about theology in the day in which we live. It revolves around the Word of God, what that Word is or isn't, and how that Word is to be interpreted or ignored. There is no neutral ground when it comes to hermeneutics. There are always presuppositions about the Word of God, a subject that will be discussed later in Chapter 3.

Hermeneutics can be likened to a large beach ball in the stands of a professional football game (especially the

San Diego Chargers) when the ball is batted into the air and is propelled around the stadium by ecstatic fans who are playing a game within a game: the beach ball game and the football game. How many games are going on? Depending on your interpretation, your hermeneutical presuppositions regarding the ball can be more than one. How far will the ball fly? How high will it ascend? Will it make the upper deck? Will a security guard confiscate it? Will it make its way onto the playing field? Then, of course, there is also the football game.

Just as the beach ball is unpredictable in the stands of a football stadium, so is hermeneutics an unpredictable theological arena. This is because man is unpredictable. The social sciences are still in the process of figuring out the intricacies of the male and female, an unending search. Theologians are likewise in an unending search regarding the interpretation of Scripture. Indeed, is it the true Word of God or simply words of an ancient culture? Is part of Scripture the Word of God and part not the Word of God? In hermeneutics, who should be doing the defining? Is it man who is the interpreter, or is God the interpreter, so that Scripture is used to interpret Scripture? This will be discussed later in Chapter 17.

I submit that everyone who has encountered Holy Scripture has had a hermeneutical encounter. He or she has an interpretation of Holy Scripture. It can run the gamut of being the inerrant and infallible Word of God in all respects, to being partially true, or entirely false, and therefore not the Word of God. It really depends upon the presuppositions of the person doing the interpreting.

What follows explores for you the flavor of what has happened and is now occurring in the hermeneutical arena, which has bearing upon your spiritual lives. As such, hermeneutics is not some ethereal word used by theologians, but a word of spiritual concern to you as well as to the clergy.

How a person interprets Holy Scripture and lives by that interpretation, has eternal implications. Yes, we know the Bible does not save us. Only Jesus Who is the center of all Scripture can do that!

CHAPTER 2

Deception . . . Confusion

Pilate said to Him, "What is truth?" (John 18:38)

You and I are "word assaulted" today. Never before in the history of man has the bombardment of words to convey ideas, positive, as well as negative, been so prolific.

Newspapers, magazines, television, radio, the Internet, and just plain everyday conversations teem with conflicting words that make our heads spin. There is that word *spin,* a word that has catapulted to prominence in the politics and ethics of the 1990s. However, *spin* as fabrication has been with mankind since the Genesis 3 account. We are numbed by the word/idea spin-onslaught. We ask, "What is truth?" just as Pilate asked. It doesn't take much effort to be confused by it all.

This confusion is not the sole property of the secular world where "everything and anything goes." It is also the theme song of the prince of darkness. This confusion has also spilled over into the Church of Jesus Christ, the body of Christ, comprised of denominations with doctrines or teachings that do not always coincide or agree.

Volumes have been written by historians of the Christian church throughout the centuries concerning how theologians have led and directed their respective churches according to their doctrinal conclusions regarding the interpretation of the Bible. Some theologians have been out front as to which portions of Holy Scripture can be trusted as being Holy Scripture, and which portions of the Scriptures can be lightly regarded or ruled out completely as being the Word of God. Yes, there is and has been biblical spin at work, and you have been influenced and affected by it.

Other theologians have embraced Holy Scripture as the inerrant and infallible Word of God. It all boils down to how much authority the Word of God has today as it is viewed by the denominations that make up the world-wide Christian church. When tradition also becomes an authority, as it does in the Roman Catholic Church, and is added to the question of the authoritative truth of God, the one who called the Christian church a "Heinz 57 Variety" wasn't far off the mark.

If anyone wants to go "church shopping" today, America has a supermarket of choices and varieties where "just the right taste" to satisfy the spiritual palate can be found. If anyone is looking for a good definition of diversity (a word that has come with impact upon the American Christian church scene), one need look no further than the doctrinal stances of Christian churches today, stances that are rooted in the way Holy Scripture is interpreted.

Is Holy Scripture the authentic Word of God, or have parts of it been chosen and other parts discarded in the formulation of Christian doctrine? Again, many voices speak and declare their doctrines or teachings. Confusion reigns.

Is this confusion a tactic of deception in which the prince of darkness delights? Is this his attack upon Jesus, especially as seen in His High Priestly Prayer?

> I do not ask in behalf of these alone, but for those also who believe in Me through their word; that they may all be one; even as Thou, Father, art in Me, and I in Thee, that they also may be in Us; that the world may believe that Thou didst send Me. And the glory which Thou hast given Me I have given to them; that they may be one, just as *We* [italics added] are one; I in them, and Thou in Me, that they may be perfected in unity, that the world may know that Thou didst send Me, and didst love them, even as Thou didst love Me. (John 17:20–23)

Most Bible commentaries agree that this portion of Christ's prayer is centered upon His love for the universal church, so that there would be unity in His Church. This unity, however, has not been realized as we see variations of interpretations of the Word of God in Scripture. No doubt, this confuses you. "How come?" you ask. "Why are we not all on the same page of God's all-powerful Word to His people?" You know that our Lord is not a Lord of confusion and that He wants unity as His prayer declares. So, from where does the confusion come? Could it be that it comes from an attack on Holy Scripture as the Word of God by the prince of darkness, or does the attack emanate in biblical scholars who have a better idea than God concerning Scripture? In either scenario, the Messenger has been attacked.

In politics today, there is a tactic that goes like this: "Attack the messenger if the news he brings is harmful or threatening to an incumbent or to a candidate running for office." The prince of darkness used this tactic long before it became popular in the political arena. He made his way into the hearts and minds of good people, theologians who believed in God the Father, the Son, and the Holy Spirit as the Triune God. He made them question the authority of God's Word as though what they were doing was their right and obligation as scholars. Whether they intended it or not, they attacked God and His Word, the message. In so doing, they attacked Jesus. If we believe that Paul in 2 Timothy 3:15–17 has given us the purpose of the Scriptures, then to question them is an affront to Jesus.

> . . . and from childhood you have known the sacred writings which are able to give you the wisdom that leads to salvation through faith which is in Christ Jesus. All Scripture is inspired by God and profitable for teaching, for reproof, for correction, for training in righteousness; that the man of God may be adequate, equipped for every good work.

In light of the above, Paul plainly states that Holy Scripture is inspired by God and brings us to faith in Christ, teaches us truths of God, corrects us when we fall into sinful ways, informs us of the ways in which our God delights, and finally leads to salvation through that same faith in Jesus.

Would God have His beloved question His Word? Yet, questioning came to the hearts and minds of some biblical scholars as they studied the Holy Scriptures, the Word of God. Just as the prince of darkness brought confusion to God's creation by deception, so their questioning attacks Almighty God by raising doubt about the authority of His Word. Yes, "All warfare is based on deception." And we see this deception in lives like yours where the authority of God's Word may have been surrounded with doubt and uncertainty. This deception is spiritual warfare. It is God's Holy Word in Scripture that is questioned, and it is God's precious people for whom Christ died and rose again who are caught in the middle. Do you feel the pressure?

The questioning of God's Word will be addressed in Chapters 5 through 11. The questioning of God's Word, which is the questioning of His authority, remains as one of the main theological issues of our day. It will not evaporate nor go away.

Darrell Jodock, head of the religion department at Muhlenberg College, Allentown, Pennsylvania, commented upon the theological training of students at ELCA seminaries where biblical authority may have been questioned or not fully addressed. He wrote:

> More specifically, seminary training may have left clergy without an integrated view of biblical authority. . . . Their biblical studies may have habituated them to the discipline of historical-critical study, but they use the discipline without integrating it into any coherent theological outlook. They may be clear about what views of biblical authority they oppose but may be unable to explain one they endorse.[1]

The authority of Scripture or its opposite, its alienation in higher education, was the subject of the following words by J. Christian Baker in 1970:

> The strange new world of the Bible has become so strange to the average student (in our seminaries and universities) that he can no longer find the bridge between the world of meaning and the biblical world. The alienation of the Bible is the predominant issue in theology today. [2]

David F. Wells, in his book, *No Place for Truth,* wrote concerning the authority of Scripture and the place of that authority in theology:

> . . . theology is not simply a philosophical reflection about the nature of things but is rather the cogent articulation of the knowledge of God. Its substance is not drawn from mere human reflection, no matter how brilliant, but from the biblical Word by which it is nurtured and disciplined. And its purpose is not primarily to participate in the conversation of the learned but to nurture the people of God.[3]

Nurturing the people of God in the authority of the truthfulness of God's Word, may not be the way of postmodern biblical scholars. We do know that it is certainly not the objective of the prince of darkness. Deception and confusion are his tools of warfare, and the number of spiritual casualties that lie upon this world's spiritual battlefield are like unknown soldiers, their number and identity known only to God.

Notes

1. Darrell Jodock, *The Church's Bible,* (Minneapolis: Fortress Press, 1989), 2–3.
2. J. Christian Baker, "*Reflections On Biblical Theology*" in Interpretation, (July 1970), 303.
3. David F. Wells, *No Place For Truth,* (Michigan: William B. Eerdman Publishing Co., 1993), 5.

CHAPTER 3

Who Is Telling the Truth?

O send out Thy light and Thy truth, let them lead me. . . . (Ps. 43:3a)

Dr. R. C. Sproul tells a fascinating story:

The pastor of a local congregation announced good news to his people. The church was experiencing rapid growth and the church building was now too small to accommodate them. The church was located in an area where property was selling at premium prices, costing about $100,000 an acre. The building committee had tried desperately to find acreage at an affordable price, but there was no land available near the church. Time after time they had approached landowners but none was willing to sell. The pastor told the story:

"I have good news. As you know, we have prayed that God would open doors for us. We decided to approach a

> particular landowner, one last time, who has repeatedly turned us down. When we went to him, he had just experienced an unexpected turn of events with a parcel of ground. He agreed to sell it to us *and* to donate four hundred thousand dollars of the purchase price!"
>
> The pastor said it was an answer to prayer. Was it? He said that God had opened the door for the property. Had He? What happened here? Was this a case of divine providence at work, or was it merely the mortal machinations of a business deal? If there is no God, then the answer is easy—it was a sheer human deal and any appeal to Providence is a delusion. If there is a God who answers prayers, then the pastor was correct in calling his congregation to a spirit of gratitude before God.
>
> How we understand the incident depends on how we view the world we live in. It depends on whether we think God is sovereign over life, or if we think nobody is home in heaven.[1]

Two views, or perhaps many views, can center in on this story. Yet, the pivotal question regarding God remains. Was He involved, or was He an innocent bystander? Was this pure chance, or did God have His way in the life of the landowner? Where is the truth?

The story illustrates how people perceive God as "turning in the wind," so that God must be and act like the God we picture in our heart and mind. He can be constructed or destructed mentally. He either exists for us as God, or He doesn't exist at all. It depends upon our presuppositions.

As R. C. Sproul used the word *think* as the means by which the situation can be presupposed to be true or false, the noun *presupposition* takes on vibrant meaning when it is applied to Holy Scripture as the Word of God, not the Word of God, or as merely containing the Word of God.

What is our point of view regarding Holy Scripture? Is it God's Holy Word, or is it partially God's Holy Word? Are there other presupposed factors which make the "or" clause of the above stand as the correct view of God's Holy Word for our day and age?

Again, many voices speak according to their presuppositions, that which they suppose or assume beforehand to be true or false, according to their interpretation of the facts or the situation. As such, a presupposition can never be neutral. It is like a seesaw on a playground. It does not find equal balance when two people who are not equal in physical weight are on board. It will tip one way or another, depending on factors of weight and thrust. With presuppositions, nothing is equal unless the presupposition involves a neutral situation, but when one regards the Word of God and is concerned about it, neutrality can not be an option.

A presupposition is the starting point in looking at any subject, whether it is God's Word, politics, business, sports, etc. Once you know a person's presupposition, you can anticipate and know where the conclusion is heading. For example, you can usually differentiate a Republican from a Democrat by their presuppositions regarding taxes and the size of government. In the same manner, on the life issue, one can tell a pro-life advocate from a pro-abortion advocate by simply asking the following question: Does life begin at conception, or is there something ill-defined in the womb that has no semblance to life, so that it can be surgically or medically removed? How we humans can take sides according to our presuppositions!

Presuppositions are written every day in the headlines of our newspapers as well as in editorials and letters to the editor. Talk shows reek of presuppositions, as does the analysis of the news from Washington, D.C. and other parts of the globe. Simply stated, we Americans take sides. We are hardly ever neutral. We have presuppositions on almost every subject that has interest to us, and, yes, we have presuppositions regarding the Word of God in Holy Scripture.

In regard to Holy Scripture, who is telling the truth? Is Holy Scripture really the Word of God? Can that Word or word be trusted? With so much chaos and confusion in the world today, can any Word or word be trusted? Where is truth?

Since World War II, Americans have witnessed a revolution in the way truth is seen or viewed. Even before that second great war to end all wars began, there was in place the Judeo-Christian value system, which firmly held there was truth in Holy Scripture, and this truth came from God. Family life was strong, the sabbath worship of God was taken seriously and held in respect, and the Bible was read in the classrooms of America's schools. There was the presupposition that truth came from God and that His truth could be trusted for all of life.

Then came our participation in the Vietnam War in the 1960s and 1970s. Along with the turmoil that erupted in the universities regarding opposition to the war in the mid-1960s, there arose a worldview called secular humanism. Its main tenant, or belief, was the presupposition that man can not know truth as an absolute from God because God doesn't exist. It held that man is the source of truth because man makes the definitions of what is and what is not truth. Truth was now on a slippery slope. Absolute truth from God in Holy Scripture was abandoned in favor of man's wisdom and worldly accommodations to man which gave homage to man and not to God. St. Paul clarified this presupposition when he wrote in Romans 1:25: "For they exchanged the truth of God for a lie, and worshipped and served the creature rather than the Creator. . . ."

In the late 1980s, another view of truth impacted American culture and the culture of the world. It is called post-modernism. While secular humanism abandoned God and His Word in Holy Scripture as the source of truth, post-modernism went a step further. It abandoned man as the definer of truth. It maintains that there are no recognizable sources of authority. God doesn't exist, and truth can not be known as coming from man because there is no truth, only moral relativism in which there is no such thing as right or wrong.

When truth, especially God's truth in Holy Scripture, reposes in ruins in a post-modern world, the only thing that remains is possibilities, which like shoes, have to be tried on until a good fit is obtained. What fits one person as truth in a post-modern world may or may not fit another, and on and on the possibilities mount until confusion reigns. Where is truth, or what is truth? Has it disappeared, or is it now masquerading as a matter of personal choice, so that it means whatever a person wants it to mean— but it is not labeled as truth because that would presuppose that there is truth, that there is right and wrong?

David Wells clarified the presuppositions of post-modernism when he described its impact upon the world and the Church.

> The children who have grown up or are growing up in the post-modern world bear its mark. They are cut loose from everything, hollowed out, eclectic, patched together from scraps of personality picked up here and there, leery of commitments, empty of all passions except that of sex, devoid of the capacity for commitment, fixated on image rather than substance, operating on the seductive elixir of unrestricted personal preference, and informed only by personal intuition. They are sophisticates haunted by

> ominous superstitions, brittle rationalists living in the grip of outrageous myths, shifting, aching beings who gaze on the world as voyeurs and whose vision of salvation has dwindled to nothing more than hope for a fleeting sense of well-being. When these children shape a faith after their own habits, as they are doing in some evangelical churches, it does not much resemble the classic contours of historic Christianity.
>
> When the church abandons the biblical world view, when it fails to confront its culture with this world view in a cogent fashion, it has lost its nerve, its soul and its *raison d'etre*. It becomes like an English teacher who goes to China but makes only a feeble attempt to teach the language and then, out of a desperate sense of loneliness, learns Cantonese so that no one will have to speak English again.
>
> The church has no future if it chooses from weakness not to speak its own language, the language of truth and understanding, in the post-modern world. The days when the church could bumble along in the context of an essentially civil culture are gone. The choices now are sharp and clear. Which of these two competing and antagonistic loves will hold the evangelical heart: love for God or love for the world?[2]

The battle for truth has not been exhausted. There is no armistice in sight. Differing and emerging world views will try to establish their deceptions as truth. Truth will appear to be on that slippery slope of man's slide into confusion. Many casualties may sadly result, but God's truth in Jesus Christ can never be defeated, dulled, or made extinct; for you see God has the greatest presupposition of all time. John 3:16 is God's presupposition that has its roots in the words of God's Son Who was with the Father before the world was created:

> For God so loved the world, that He gave His only begotten Son, that whoever believes in Him should not perish, but have eternal life. (John 3:16)

The next chapter contains presuppositions concerning the orthodox Christian view of the Word of God.

Notes

1. R.C. Sproul, *Lifeviews,* (Old Tappan, N.J.: Fleming H. Revell Company, 1986), 24.
2. David F. Wells, *God In The Wasteland*, (Grand Rapids, Michigan: William B. Eerdmans Publishing Company; and Leicester, England: Inter-Varsity Press, 1994), 222–223.

CHAPTER 4

Word of God, Its Meaning

For the word of God is living and active and sharper than any two-edged sword, and piercing as far as the division of soul and spirit, of both joints and marrow, and able to judge the thoughts and intentions of the heart. (Heb. 4:12)

If theology is the study of God and His relation to the world, then God's Word becomes the foundation, the basis for that study. Yet today, there are differing definitions given to the Word of God. Some theologians point to the Bible and allow the Bible to define the Word of God. Others extract Jesus as the only definition worthy of being called the "Word of God," and say that the Bible does not have the authority of being propositional truth from God, inspired by His Spirit. We will see this position by Semler (later in Chapter 7) who could not equate all Scripture as being Word of God, and by Barth (in Chapter 9,) who could give no authority to the Bible as being true Word of God. My stance is that of honoring Holy Scripture as the reference because the ultimate source is God Himself. It is His Word!

In the Old Testament, as well as the New Testament, we see the Word of God as power. In Genesis 1:3, we encounter God speaking His Word as creation power and might:

> Then God said, "Let there be light" and there was light.

Psalm 33:6 declares:

> By the word of the Lord the heavens were made, and by the breath of His mouth all their host.

And again in Isaiah 55:11:

> So shall My word be which goes forth from My mouth: It shall not return to Me empty, without accomplishing what I desire, and without succeeding in the matter for which I sent it.

In the New Testament, Acts 6:7 states:

> And the word of God kept on spreading, and the number of the disciples continued to increase greatly in Jerusalem, and a great many of the priests were becoming obedient to the faith.

John 5:24 pronounces and echoes the power of the Word as our Lord declared it:

> Truly, truly, I say to you, he who hears My word, and believes Him who sent Me, has eternal life, and does not come into judgment, but has passed out of death into life.

Power, God's power in creation, as well as salvation in and through faith in Jesus, has been the joy and song of God's people who live in His Word.

There is a second understanding of the Word of God, again in the New Testament, which is expressed as *logos* in the Greek. John 1:1–14 has emblazoned upon the hearts of God's people the truth that Jesus is the Living Word of God, the Incarnate Word, God in human flesh. "In the beginning was the Word, and the Word was with God, and the Word was God. He was in the beginning with God." These and following verses declare Jesus as the Living Word of God.

As the New Testament witness to Jesus as God's Word comes to a close, there is that final hammer of the nail of truth, which is written in Revelation 19:13:

> And He is clothed with a robe dipped in blood; and His name is called the Word of God.

A third understanding of the Word of God that most Christians can easily accept is the Word of God as Holy Scripture. It refers to the entire content of the Bible. It is that which God's Holy Spirit caused to be written or spoken as God's Word to His people. In Jeremiah 30:1–3, we read:

> The word which came to Jeremiah from the Lord, "Thus says the Lord, the God of Israel, 'Write all the words which I have spoken to you in a book. For behold, days are coming, declares the Lord, when I will restore the fortunes of My people Israel and Judah.' The Lord says, 'I will also bring them back to the land that I gave to their forefathers, and they shall possess it.'"

In 2 Peter 1:19–21 we read:

> And so we have the prophetic word made more sure, to which you do well to pay attention as to a lamp shining in a dark place, until the day dawns and the morning star arises in your hearts. But know this first of all, that no prophecy of Scripture is a matter of one's interpretation, for no prophecy was ever made by an act of human will, but men moved by the Holy Spirit spoke from God.

In the scriptural context of the above quote, Dr. Robert D. Preus has written:

> Scripture is not God's Word merely in the sense that God providentially uses men's thoughts and words and makes them His own. Scripture is not God's Word merely in the sense that it successfully conveys a message of God to man, but Scripture is itself God's message to man. . . . we have seen that Lutheran theology calls Scripture the Word of God because of a present action, that God today and always works through Scripture. According to its very nature (forma), Scripture is the Word of God.[1]

A fourth understanding of the Word of God is that it is eternal. Psalm 119:89 declares:

> Forever, O Lord, Thy word is settled in heaven.

God's word never will be changed; and again in verse 160 of that psalm:

> The sum of Thy word is truth, And every one of Thy righteous ordinances is everlasting.

Jesus, in Matthew 24:35 said, "Heaven and earth will pass away, but My words shall not pass away." And Peter in his first epistle, chapter 1, verse 25, quoted Isaiah 40:8: "BUT THE WORD OF THE LORD ABIDES FOREVER."

As Holy Scripture, the Bible is revelation; revelation of our God making known through the power of the Holy Spirit what otherwise would be unknown had He not first revealed it to us. This revelation comes as both Law and Gospel, His Word for us who are His beloved. The Law of God convicts us of our sinful nature, and the Gospel proclaims what Jesus has done to save sinners like you and me from eternal death and condemnation. The Gospel is good news because of the authority of Scripture.

The four basic concepts of the Word of God which I have defined, can be expanded upon by theologians who want to give God the blessing and honor of His Word, or they can be attacked by those theologians who want to redefine the Word of God according to their intellectual prowess of reason.

The one constant, however, in today's theological scene is that the Word of God is a target in the on-going saga of biblical scholarship which, like the sea on which I sailed as a Navy chaplain, was in constant motion. Theologians who target God's Word for attack and deception—yes, there is that word *deception*—will be discussed, not in the totality of their work of biblical criticism because of space. Examples of their work will be presented as a flavor of their confusion and deception regarding the Word of God, which I believe, has not brought blessing and honor to God's Word. Instead, it has encouraged confusion and deception, a most favorite tactic of God's enemy. I believe these theologians were sincere in their actions and thoughts as they dug deep by means of their scholarly prowess and took apart the Word of God, so that they could present—could it be—a clearer meaning to the Word of God?

Nevertheless, the meaning of the Word of God has been not only a target, but a tennis ball that has been volleyed across the net of truth by those who defend Holy Scripture as the Word of God, as well as by those who would dissect and judge it according to man's standards of reason and man's scholarship criteria. Again, it is many voices speaking. Who is telling the truth? Where is the blessing? Where is the honor?

Notes

1. Robert D. Preus, *The Theology of Post-Reformation Lutheranism*, (St. Louis: Concordia Publishing House, 1970), 265.

CHAPTER 5

Questioning the Word of God

Jesus answered and said to him, "If anyone loves me, he will keep My word; and My Father will love him, and We will come to him, and make our abode with him. He who does not love Me does not keep My words, and the word which you hear is not Mine, but the Father's who sent Me." (John 14:23, 24)

Christians like you who attend worship and hear sermons on texts from the Bible, or attend Bible study classes, are very rarely aware of how Holy Scripture as God's Word has and is being questioned. Of course, there will be exceptions. However, any questioning of the authority of God's Word could cause an uproar in most Christian congregations. It would be taken as an attack against God. Preachers have been known to preface their sermons with these words: "What we have here in our text is a mystery." Or they may raise a slight question as to what Saint Paul or Saint Peter really means in the appointed text of the sermon, but they will hardly ever make a direct frontal attack in questioning God's Word.

For the most part, worshipers depart from their churches with happy grins and thank the preacher for a "good sermon," "a sermon that provoked thought," or "Your sermon really spoke to me today." or "Do you think the Eagles will beat the Redskins?"

The every-Sunday worshiper in Christian churches around the world is unaware of the battle concerning the Word of God. This battle has been kept within the walls of theological academia for years. The spiritual implications and consequences of that battle hang heavily upon Christian denominations today and will be discussed later in Chapter 13. Where there is battle, there is confusion and deception, and there are also casualties. Every battle has them, and this one is no exception.

As a youth growing up in Philadelphia, who attended church twice a Sunday, served as an acolyte (the one "who turns on and off" the candles on the altar), and one who felt and knew in his heart the call to the Christian ministry, I loved Holy Scripture as God's Word. My pastors never gave me cause to question that Holy Word. Yet, upon arriving at the Lutheran Theological Seminary at Philadelphia in the fall of 1954, one of my first encounters, which shocked me, were words from a professor stating that "We are going to do away with your Sunday School faith and build you into a mature faith."

Wow! Was I now being made privy to some sort of special spiritual blessing or gift because I was within the hallowed walls and halls of seminary? Was this seminary experience going to give me a higher level of understanding what faith is about? Was this going to be like a fraternity initiation, this eventual initiation into the clergy? Was I about to stand closer to God than I had ever been before?

What I encountered in regard to God's Word was the historical-critical method of biblical interpretation, a method that has its beginning or roots in an eighteenth century phenomenon called the Enlightenment. Walter Wink, in a book published in 1973 by Fortress Press (the publishing company linked to the ELCA), stated quite frankly that the historical-critical method was a tool or a means by which seminary students could be weaned away, separated from conservative views of Holy Scripture, so that they would embrace liberal theology.

> Far more fundamentally than revivalism, biblical criticism shook, shattered, and reconstituted generation after generation of students, and became their point of entree unto the "modern world".[1]

Theodore Tappert, in his 100th anniversary history of the Lutheran Theological Seminary at Philadelphia from 1864 to 1964, revealed the place of the historical-critical method in the seminary's biblical objective.

> The theology taught in the seminary during the quarter of a century between 1938 and 1964 may be characterized as historical in its orientation, but not in the sense in which this had been true before. The ecclesiastical heritage continued to be respected but it was no longer looked upon as normative. On the one hand, this heritage was not seen in the same light as before. It was subjected to re-examination, and earlier views about it were in certain respects altered. This applies not only to the immediate heritage of the Lutheran Church in the United States but also to the larger Reformation tradition, and indeed to the whole Christian past, including the Scriptures themselves. . . . The seminary participated

in the revived interest in theology, which was generally characteristic of this period. Its teaching was influenced in various ways by the Luther renaissance, by new biblical studies, by existentialism, by the ecumenical movement, by new social awareness.[2]

Rather than present a lengthy description of the historical-critical method as might be written for a theologian, I will unfold the development so that it is understandable to you, the lay person. But first, some insights about the historical-critical method.

It was an indisputable truth that until the end of the seventeenth century, almost all Christians believed that what was contained in the writings of the Old and New Testaments was the inspired, infallible, inerrant Word of God. With the advent of the Enlightenment in the eighteenth century, the inspiration, along with the infallibility and inerrancy of Holy Scripture, were questioned and attacked.

Van A. Harvey wrote:

> As Gerhard Ebling has pointed out, the entire history of Christian theology may be regarded as the history of Biblical interpretation. This is especially true of Protestant theology, because it has been characterized from the outset by appeal to the Bible as the sole norm of faith and practice (*sola scriptura*). It is just for this reason that Biblical criticism poses such a fateful problem for the Protestant community. It not only raises questions concerning the truth of historical narratives, but it materially affects the reading of Scripture itself by posing the question of interpretation and meaning.[3]

The historical-critical method, as it developed in the eighteenth century and continues to this day, has been built on the presupposition of man's authority of interpretation of the Scriptures over God's authority in His Holy Word. It is without a doubt a divisive issue, dividing denomination from denomination, according to the doctrines or dogmas they proclaim as they interpret the Bible as the inerrant, inspired Word of God, as simply containing the Word of God, or as an ancient text that has to be newly fathomed by scholars to extract the "meaningful" Word of God for the contemporary scene.

Today a deep divide exists between the ELCA and the LCMS. While they both bear the name *Lutheran*, they regard the Holy Scriptures differently. The former embraces the historical-critical method of biblical interpretation, while the latter does not. My position throughout this book centers on the confusion and deception, which this method produces. I know many who in good faith believe this to be the correct method to be employed in hermeneutics. My disagreement is with their conclusion. I only hope and pray that some day we will be in agreement that Scripture is the inerrant and infallible Word of God.

The historical-critical method presupposes that the Bible was a creation of both God and man, in that it contained a divine word and a human word. Thus, there was God/man cooperation. The problem then arises in determining what part of Scripture comes from God and what part comes from man. While any errors could be laid upon man, the larger task was to authenticate what could be true revelation from God, and thus honored as the Word of God.

In Chapter 7 we will meet Johann Salomo Semler, regarded by many as the father of the historical-critical method. As we see this method unfold in the theologians that follow, we will see in some of them the cooperative premise that Scripture is both the Word of God and word of man.

Harvey regarded Ernst E. P. Troeltsch, a German Lutheran theologian who lived from 1865 to 1923, as one who clearly defined the historical-critical method. Troeltsch was firmly committed to this method. He maintained it was the only option for the Christian church in its quest to tell what could be nailed down in Scripture as scientific fact and which could be equated as truth. The method as Harvey interpreted Troeltsch, could be compared to a drive conditioned by a will-to-truth. Harvey wrote:

> This will-to-truth became attached to the method, and the presuppositions of that method, Troeltsch concluded, were basically incompatible with traditional Christian faith, based as it ultimately is on a supernaturalistic metaphysics. This incompatibility was most clearly seen, he thought, in the realm of Biblical criticism. The problem was not, as many theologians then believed, that the Biblical critics emerged from their libraries with results disturbing to believers, but that the method itself, which led to those results, was based on assumptions quite irreconcilable with traditional belief. If the theologian regards the Scriptures as supernaturally inspired, the historian must assume that the Bible is intelligible only in terms of its historical context and is subject to the same principles of interpretation and criticism that are applied to other ancient literature. If the theologian believes that the events of the Bible are the results of the supernatural intervention of God, the historian regards such an explanation as a hindrance to true historical understanding. If the theologian believes that the events upon which Christendom rests are unique, the historian assumes that these events, like all events, are analogous to those in the present and that it is only on this assumption that statements about them can be assessed at all. If the theologian believes on faith that certain events occurred, the

> historian regards all historical claims as having only a greater or lesser degree of probability, and he regards the attachment of faith to these claims as a corruption of historical judgment.[4]

If the claims of the orthodox theologian are false concerning God and His truth as the Bible states, that the Bible is not completely the Word of God, then faith has no foundation whatsoever. The doubt of the critic or the historian must now prevail, as he reconstructs according to historical principles what he believes to be historically palatable. Simply put, doubt becomes a virtue, and faith, a sin. Is this not confusion and deception concerning the Word of God?

Most members of a Christian denomination or church understand that atheists and agnostics (terms that are roughly synonymous of each other) attack God's Word and call it into question at every opportunity, but would Christian scholars do that to God's Word? Such a practice over two hundred years ago would have appeared to be incredible. Yet, today we see such attacks, which bring confusion upon the people of God in many Christian churches.

The confusion comes because the authority of the Word of God has been deflated and abandoned, so that absolutes in Scripture as the Word of God not only have been neutered but also rendered as "archaic." If the Word of God is not an absolute truth, where does one find absolute truth? The Word of God, since the Enlightenment, has been like a soccer ball, booted to and fro by biblical scholars who use the historical-critical method. Theological consensus is now a pipe-dream, except for those who believe that the authority of man supersedes the authority of God's Word in Holy Scripture, and even they can not always agree.

Martin Luther in his 1535 Lectures on Galatians stated:

> Therefore let us learn that this is one of the devil's specialties: If he cannot do his damage by persecuting and destroying, he will do it under the guise of correcting and edifying.[5]

And that is exactly the tactic of the historical-critical method of biblical interpretation. It takes what has stood for centuries as God's Word, and as a judge, brings "correction and edification" to it, as would a "reasonable, intelligent scholar."

Notes

1. Walter Wink, *The Bible in Human Transformation,* (Philadelphia: Fortress Press, 1973), 15.
2. Theodore Tappert, *History of The Lutheran Theological Seminary at Philadelphia 1864-1964* (Philadelphia Lutheran Theological Seminary, 1964), 122.
3. Van A. Harvey, *The Historian & The Believer,* (Philadelphia: Westminster Press, 1966) 19.
4. Ibid., 4–5.
5. Martin Luther, *Lectures on Galatians -1533*, trans. J. Pelikan, Luther's Works, (St. Louis: Concordia Publishing House, 1963), vol.26, 50.

CHAPTER 6

The Impact of the Enlightenment

"Is not My Word like fire?" declares the Lord, "and like a hammer which shatters a rock?" (Jer. 23:29)

The Enlightenment, which began in the eighteenth century, is also called the "Age of Reason." It brought to the forefront man and the capacity of his reason as competent authority. The church, the Bible, and the state—as figures of authority—were questioned. Philosophy and science rose on the wings of reason. Prior to the Enlightenment, religious truth was regarded as coming from God's revelation of Himself in Holy Scripture. From the Enlightenment to the day in which we now live, religious truth coming from God's revelation is seen as no longer able to provide objective information, the truth, about man or the universe in which he lives. A new source of truth had been found in the natural, historical, and social sciences.

One of the clearest definitions of the Enlightenment is found in *The Dictionary of the Christian Church.*

> The Enlightenment combines opposition to all supernatural religion and belief in the all-sufficiency of human reason with an ardent desire to promote the happiness of men in this life. . . . Most of its representatives . . . rejected the Christian dogma and were hostile to Catholicism as well as Protestant orthodoxy, which they regarded as powers of spiritual darkness, depriving humanity of the use of its rational faculties. . . . Their fundamental belief in the goodness of human nature, which blinded them to the fact of sin, produced an easy optimism and absolute faith of human society once the principles of enlightened reason had been recognized. The spirit of the Enlightenment penetrated deeply into German Protestantism (in the 19th century), where it disintegrated faith in the authority of the Bible and encouraged Biblical criticism on the one hand and an emotional "Pietism" on the other.[1]

David F. Wells gave a realistic appraisal of the Enlightenment.

> The Enlightenment world liberated us to dream dreams of the world's renovation and of ourselves at its center, standing erect and proud, recasting the whole sorry scheme of things bare-handed, as it were leaning only on our own reason and goodness. It also liberated us to perceive illusion as reality. . . . The real outcome of the Enlightenment, however, has not been the preservation of noble values but their collapse into complete relativism. . . . There is violence on earth. The liberated search only for power. Industry despoils the earth. The powerful ride roughshod over the weak. The poor are left to die on street grates. The unborn are killed before they can ever see the rich and beautiful world that God made. The elderly are encouraged to get on with the business of dying so that we

> may take their places. . . . Although the brazen promises of the Enlightenment about the possibility of remaking all of life are now dead, the premises on which they were built—freedom from God, freedom from authority, freedom from the past, freedom from evil—simply refuses to die.[2]

Something else happened during the Enlightenment. Prior to it, there was an even balance in the way God was proclaimed and comprehended in faith. He was looked to as our transcendent God, the creator of the world, uniquely different from His creation, eternal, unchanging, holy, righteous, and the epitome of love. Yet, at the same time, He was immanently involved in the affairs of man who was created in His image whereby man has the capacity to love and be loved. The former can be defined as the transcendence of God, while the later is the immanence of God.

In both, His transcendence and immanence, God sent His Son, Jesus, into the world. In His transcendence, only God can send His Son, born of a virgin, to this earth for man's salvation. In His immanence, God can be known in faith by those who believe in His Son, yet He intimately loves even those who do not love His Son as their Lord and Redeemer. He reaches out to them through witness to the Word of God by believers, who honor the working of the Holy Spirit and the testimony of the Holy Spirit's work in their own lives. The Christian church, His body, is living reality of His immanence here on earth. Matthew 18:20 declares these words of Jesus: "For where two or three have gathered together in My name, there I am in their midst." The transcendence and the immanence of God were held in balance prior to the Enlightenment. But then, something else happened.

That something else was the emergence of man as his own defining god, who could reason for himself, construct a world that is meaningful to his tastes and appetites, bring in the whole realm of nature, look at it scientifically, and explain creation as well as salvation in his own "godly" terms. The absolutes of God in Holy Scripture and the teachings, or dogma, that came from God's Word took back seat to man's reason, his autonomy, and his mastery of nature through science. Thus, there was a shift in world views. The balance between the transcendence of God and His immanence was gone. "Reasonable" man left God to His heaven and now looked within himself and his world for ultimate meaning. "Reasonable" man brought God to dwell in *his* definition of immanence. This will become evident as we consider theologians committed to the historical-critical method of biblical interpretation.

Edgar Krentz, a proponent of the historical-critical method, tells what this method has done (and what it is) as it developed from the eighteenth century into the nineteenth century.

> It is difficult to overestimate the significance the nineteenth century has for biblical interpretation. It made historical criticism *the* approved method of interpretation. The result was a revolution of viewpoint in evaluating the Bible. The Scriptures were, so to speak, secularized. The biblical books became historical documents to be studied and questioned like any other ancient sources. The Bible was no longer the criterion for the writing of history; rather history had become the criterion for understanding the Bible. The variety in the Bible was highlighted; its unity had to be discovered and could no longer be presumed. The history it reported was no longer assumed to be everywhere correct. The Bible stood before criticism as defendant before judge.[3]

The Bible, the Word of God, as the defendant? Man as the judge? Man standing in judgment over the Word of God? Could Martin Luther ever conceive that this juxtaposition would ever occur?

Indeed, the deeper and more insightful questions are: Would our Lord Jesus ever consent to the created (man) having authority over the Creator's Holy Word? Is the mind of man far superior to the mind and heart of His Creator? In all of this, the burning question remains: Can God give His blessing and honor to such a situation? The answer from Holy Scripture is most obvious. Isaiah 55:10–11 gives such an answer.

> For as the rain and the snow come down from heaven, And do not return there without watering the earth, And making it bear and sprout, And furnishing seed to the sower and bread to the eater; So shall My word be which goes forth from My mouth; It shall not return to Me empty, Without accomplishing what I desire, And without succeeding in the matter for which I sent it.

Holy Scripture does not need to be defended. It needs only to be proclaimed as God's Word to His beloved. A love story doesn't have to be made into a mystery!

Yet, the questions in your mind might be: How did this come about? Yes, the Enlightenment attempted to make man's reason dominant over God's revelation in His Word, but how did it happen? Who were the main players in this saga? What did man do so that he could stand as judge over the Word of God?

When the Enlightenment occurred, another movement had already been in progress. It was called "Pietism." Philipp Jakob Spener is known as the father of Pietism. He was called to be the senior minister in Frankfurt am Main in 1666. He called for a reform, as he saw serious issues of spiritual decline in Germany. He emphasized salvation as regeneration, which was new birth obtained by both faith and works. Spener did not rely on justification by faith alone, which is at the heart of the Reformation. Pietism allowed man to become a player in his own salvation. In theology, this is called synergism wherein man works in cooperation with God for his salvation.

Evangelical Dictionary of Theology brings an insight worthy of consideration regarding the influences of Pietism:

> Historians have long studied the relationship between pietism and the Enlightenment, that rationalistic and humanistic movement which flourished during the eighteenth century and which contributed to the eventual secularization of Europe. They have noted that pietism and the Enlightenment both attacked Protestant orthodoxy, that both asserted the rights of individuals, and that both were concerned about practice more than theory. The crucial historical question is whether pietistic antitraditionalism, individualism, and practicality paved the way for a non-Christian expression of these same traits in the Enlightenment. . . . It is probably best to regard pietism as a movement that paralleled the Enlightenment and later European developments in its quest for personal meaning and its disdain for exhausted traditions. Yet insofar as the heart of pietism was captive to the gospel, it remained a source of distinctly Christian renewal.[4]

The historical-critical method of biblical interpretation did not just suddenly appear on the scene in terms of what has been described above. It had as its cradle, so to speak, the Pietism and Enlightenment forces, which emphasized breaking with the traditions of Christian orthodoxy, placing the reason of man as final authority or judge, free from external authority, free from the authority of the church, the Bible, and even the state.

Harrisville and Sundberg offer another interesting explanation why spiritual warfare and confusion have come upon the Christian church. They do so by contrasting the worldviews of Augustianism and the Enlightenment. The identity of the Christian church of the west, and especially the Protestantism of the Lutheran and Reformed churches, was dependent upon the theology of Augustine who lived from 354 to 430 A.D.

Augustianism emphasized man's sinfulness as Genesis 3 describes. As such, man can not have a right relationship with God by means of his own effort. He needs the divine grace of God in Jesus Christ in order to live. This means that God, Himself, intervenes by His Son, Jesus, and overcomes the sin of man. Augustine's famous words that "man is restless until he finds his rest in God" undergirds the Augustinian tradition, which in turn, had great influence on Martin Luther and the other Reformers of the sixteenth century. In this tradition, ultimate truth is Christian doctrine that comes from God through the Bible. The truthfulness of the Bible was paramount.

Harrisville and Sundberg wrote:

> The doctrinal crisis of Western Christianity is the clash of Augustianism with this new world view. Where Augustianism teaches that human nature is corrupted by the Fall, the Enlightenment asserts boldly the innocence of human nature. When Augustianism professes that salvation requires the direct intervention of God to rescue humanity from the sorrows of the world, the Enlightenment declares that the end of existence is the good life on earth. For Augustianism humanity stands

> under the sovereignty of God's election. In the view of the Enlightenment, humanity is capable of directing its own fate. Augustianism affirms trust in the church and the Scriptures; they provide knowledge of the truth for individual life. The Enlightenment counters that truth is obtained by pursuing critical knowledge and obtaining freedom from superstition and oppressive institutions. . . . What we are dealing with here is not a simple either/or, but a complex debate about the range of deeply held theological, philosophical, and political assumptions. Indeed, it is no exaggeration to say that the history of modern Protestant theology since the Enlightenment is the warfare between these two world views. This warfare has broken out again and again on many fronts. Historical-critical study of the Bible is only one of them; but perhaps the most important one. Peace does not appear at hand.[5]

"Theological, philosophical, and political assumptions," as stated above, provide the setting for the courtroom in which Holy Scripture has been put on trial and questioned. James Barr provided such a courtroom.

> In the heyday of the revival of biblical authority, it was apparently supposed that the authority of the Bible was in fact the key to its right interpretation, that if one accepted it as authoritative, this fact would guide one to the right exegesis. (Exegesis: an explanation or an interpretation of a text. Webster's Ninth New Collegiate Dictionary, my insertion.) Quite the contrary is the case. Only when we give up the futile expectation that the Bible's utterances will express what is right and authoritative can we begin to face it for what it really is, something belonging to an environment entirely different from our own, in which the questions and answers were entirely different.[6]

Assumptions, clear assumptions, are thrown against God's Word in Scripture, and they attempt to tear down the authority of Scripture by making Scripture something limited to the past, archaic, outdated, but which can be revived, brought to new life and meaning, by enlightened scholars who sit in judgment on God's Word.

Many scholars state their case in biblical courtrooms, more commonly than not, known as seminaries. From the seminaries come the pastors, the ministers, who are apt to "parrot" their mentors. You, the people in the pews, may hear the subtle suggestions and innuendoes concerning how Scripture must be reinterpreted in light of new scholarship, and you are confused. Very seldom is there a frontal attack on Scripture. That would send parishioners running to the exits and that would mean financial disaster. However, God's Word as you have known it from years past, is not flatly denied, but a subtle question mark is raised over its authority and meaning. The "greased pig" of pulpit proclamation and teaching surfaces as spiritual "mush," not the diet needed by you and other people of God, who come in worship to be fed with the absolute truth of God's Word.

It appears as cleverness, and it is enticing in a world that likes new innovations. The authority of Scripture is lowered, not one peg, but many pegs—if not discarded totally—in favor of the scholar or scholars who presume to rescue the truth of Scripture from the "old way" of regarding Scripture as the Word of God, now proposing that it merely "contains" the Word of God. Then, it can be brought to a meaning that is compatible with post-modern relativism where confusion reigns and God's Word in Scripture is questioned as truth from God. The question mark is one of the enemy's favorite weapons.

Notes

1. F.L. Cross, ed., *The Dictionary of the Christian Church*, (London: Oxford University Press, 1958), 104–105.
2. David F. Wells, op. cit., 57–58.
3. Edgar Krentz, *The Historical-Critical Method*, (Philadelphia: Fortress Press, 1975), 30.
4. Walter A. Elwell, ed., *Evangelical Dictionary of Theology*, (Grand Rapids, Michigan: Baker Book House, 1984), 857.
5. Roy A. Harrisville and Walter Sundberg, *The Bible in Modern Culture*, (Grand Rapids: William B. Eerdmans Publishing Company, 1995), 28–31.
6. James Barr, *The Bible In The Modern World*, (New York: Harper & Row Publishers, 1973), 43.

Chapter 7

Questioning the Word of God—Semler to Schleiermacher

And for this reason we also constantly thank God that when you received from us the Word of God's message, you accepted it not as the word of men, but for what it really is, the Word of God, which also performs its work in you who believe. (1 Thess. 2:13)

Semler

The one who has been named as the father, or the moving force, of the historical-critical method, is Johann Salomo Semler. He was born in 1725 in Saalfeld, Thuringia, the son of a Lutheran pietist pastor. His relationship with his father was not the best, and he came to abhor pietism and the orthodoxy of his father. He rose to be the head of the theological faculty at Halle. As a theologian, he challenged the divine inspiration of the Bible and maintained that the Bible was no different from any other book.

Gerhard Maier pointed out that the central principle of thought that Semler advanced, which became the motivational heart of the historical-critical method, is found in one sentence he wrote: "The root of evil (in theology) is the interchangeable use of the terms 'Scripture' and 'Word of God'".[1] He did not sanction using these terms as equals since he maintained that not all of Scripture was the Word of God. He saw as his task the challenge of finding what could be the Word of God in Scripture.

What Semler did was an attempt to shatter the authority of Holy Scripture. By placing a divide, or a wedge, between Scripture and the Word of God, he was free to be the authority and could make definitions according to his scholarship. He opened the floodgates for other theologians to pour through, to advance their own personal theories where some portions of Holy Scripture contain the Word of God, and others do not.

Just as Forest Evashevski, in 1939 and 1940, was the blocking back who helped to make Tom Harmon of Michigan an all-American football running back, so Johann Salomo Semler was the blocking back for the historical-critical method of biblical interpretation. He opened the holes through which poured the attack upon God's Holy Word in Scripture. He unleashed a hailstorm of questions and speculations. When Scripture could be separated, and not be equated as the Word of God, the Enlightenment theological academia, not limited to the eighteenth century but inclusive of nineteenth and twentieth century historical-critical theologians, became like frenzied sharks, trying to rip and tear apart God's Word.

Kant

One who threw bait, or chum, into the waters to help cause that frenzy was Immanuel Kant, who lived from 1724 to 1804. In him the zenith of the Enlightenment was reached. His influence on theology extends far beyond the eighteenth century and into the nineteenth and twentieth centuries and, perhaps, well beyond into future centuries, "if" the historical-critical method remains a backbone of liberalism.

Kant rejected metaphysical knowledge, meaning that he rejected any transcendent thought of God wherein God is the revealer of His love and will for mankind. Kant was a catalyst who put the spotlight on man as the interpreter of authority. God was pushed back into the shadows, as was His Holy Word in Scripture. It was man's ability to reason, to use his mind, which mattered. As such, man could be the definer of moral precepts, precepts that had their origin in the mind of man.

Man and his reason were raised and elevated above the Holy Scriptures and the creeds of Christendom. God, as an object of man's quest for spiritual truth, held little relevance. It was man as the subject of truth that mattered. Kant's system of philosophy confiscated and passed the mantle of authority away from God and His revelation in Holy Scripture, to the autonomy of man's reason. As such, man had no need to look to God and His revelation in Holy Scripture. God was no longer the object of man's search for meaning and direction. Man instead, became the subject of morality, as well as its definer.

Kant's story is a move, or a shift, from the divine to the ridiculous. The authority of a transcendent God lay in an ash heap before man, who dared to think for himself, because he is rational and can use the authority of his mind.

Van A. Harvey provided this insight into Immanuel Kant:

> Immanuel Kant identified enlightenment with autonomy. Enlightenment, he wrote, is man's release from all authority that would deprive him of his freedom to think without direction from another. Contrary to some

> interpretations of the Enlightenment, it was not characterized by a naive confidence in man's actual rationality. Kant's essay is not devoted to the proposition that men are rational; it is, rather, a revolutionary call for men to throw off the chains of a brutish existence and dare to think. Kant did not believe that enlightenment was common or even easily achieved among men. We do not live in an enlightened age, he wrote, but in an age of enlightenment. And it was just because he believed men found thinking for themselves difficult and dangerous that he found it necessary to issue a manifesto. "Have the courage to use your own reason" was his declaration of independence against every authority that rests on the dictatorial command, "Obey, don't think." From the standpoint of the twentieth century, it requires an act of historical imagination to conceive of the magnitude of the revolution Kant called for and that was finally realized. It required nothing less than a transformation of the intellectual ideal that had possessed the heart of Christendom for centuries, the ideal of *belief*. Kant celebrated the will-to-truth more than the will-to-believe, investigation more than certainty, autonomy more than obedience to authority.[2]

Now, in philosophy and theology, the very basis for meaning has been separated, or divorced, from that which is objective, so that meaning has become the arena for the subjective interpretations of man. It is a Tower of Babel experience on a worldwide scale, where many voices speak so that confusion reigns. Objective truth that is in the Word of God can now be questioned and called "un-truth," or whatever man deems to call it, because it is open to the subjective interpretation of man via the authority of reason, authenticated by his own autonomy. As Krentz stated so clearly in a previous quote: "The Bible stood before criticism as defendant before judge."

Lessing

A contemporary of Semler and Kant was Gotthold Ephraim Lessing who lived from 1729 to 1781. He distinguished himself as a writer, a critic, and a dramatist. He published fragments of a manuscript that had been written by Hermann Samuel Reimarus, which denied the truthfulness of biblical revelation because it could not stand up to investigation. The rationalism of the Enlightenment was alive in Lessing, because the reason of man was, for him, the defining factor in the search for truth.

Lessing made two pronouncements that have ricocheted off the walls of hermeneutical investigation from his time to this day. These pronouncements point to what has been termed as "Lessing's broad, ugly ditch," a divide, or gap, between that which is historical and that which can be known with the certainty of reason as truth. He held that if no historical truth can be demonstrated, then nothing can be demonstrated by means of historical truth. To believe, one must see and verify.

In essence, he was questioning, so as to sow doubt whether or not faith can be tied to, and connected with, historical events; events in the Bible such as the miracles of Jesus, His Resurrection, and the rest of His ministry as the Son of God in human flesh. Therefore, any and all statements regarding any historical facts in Jesus' life are statements of probability. The same can be said about any and all historical events in the Old and New Testament. God, as the exclusive revealer of His truth to man, is denied the broad sweep of the events of history in which His revelation unfolds.

Lessing's presupposition that absolute truth can not be grounded in history, let alone in Scripture, has had lasting theological repercussions, which will be seen in the theologians who embrace the historical-critical method of biblical interpretation.

Lessing's two famous statements were:

> There is a broad, ugly ditch of history that I can not jump across; and, The accidental truths of history can never become the proof of the necessary truths of reason.[3]

Alasdair I. C. Heron, concerning Lessing, has stated:

> In focusing thus sharply on the question of the relation between religious faith and historical knowledge, Lessing put his finger on what was to prove a more or less permanently controversial topic in theology from his day to this. Like Kant, he leaves theologians with two broad choices; either to accept this account of the situation, with its absolute distinction between the relativities and contingencies of history and the truth of religion, or to search for some other framework within which to set up the question. The chief motive which would naturally encourage Christian thinkers to look for such an alternative is that Lessing's horizon necessarily scales down to merely relative and passing significance the events on which Christian faith itself depends—the history recorded and interpreted in the Bible, and in particular that of Jesus himself. The last two centuries have brought a variety of attempts in theology to cope with these questions, and both alternatives bequeathed by Lessing have been followed.[4]

It may be a good idea to take a break once in a while, as these theories of theologians and philosophers are presented. They follow so closely and are inter-related to each other and to the Enlightenment. Enlightenment thought is contagious and seductive in leading man away from God to "man as god." Up to this point, it is obvious, I believe, that you can see the departure from the orthodox position, which clearly states that Scripture is the Word of God.

As a breather, some words from Martin Luther apply as we move forward to see the impact of some well-meaning theologians, who apparently did not hear, or chose to disregard, Luther's godly wisdom.

> Let him who wants to study theology and become proficient in it be a fool. Then he will be a theologian. The most important art of a future theologian is to distinguish very carefully between the wisdom of reason and that of the Word or the knowledge of God. The folk who confuse those are mixing heaven with earth.[5]

Hegel

A German philosopher by the name of George Wilhelm Freidrich Hegel, who lived from 1770 to 1831, and thus followed closely in time when Kant's teachings were being widely regarded and accepted as truth, continues to this day to have influence on modern theology and on the historical-critical method. Carl E. Braaten, one of the leading theologians of the ELCA, points to both Kant and Hegel as influencing present-day theology. He wrote:

> We are yet in the situation of presiding over the synthesis of Christianity and modernity that took its shape from the Enlightenment. This is why the philosophies of Kant and Hegel continue to exercise so much influence in present-day theology.[6]

Francis Schaeffer defined one of the major influences Hegel had on theology when he quoted part of a summary from Frederick Copleston regarding Hegel.

> "According to Hegel, the universe is steadily unfolding and so is man's understanding of it. No single proposition about reality can truly reflect what is the case. Rather, in the heart of the truth of a given proposition one finds its opposite. This, where recognized, unfolds and stands in opposition to the thesis. Yet there is truth in both thesis and antithesis, and when this is perceived a synthesis is formed and a new proposition states the truth of the newly recognized situation. But this in turn is found to contain its own contradiction and the process goes on ad infinitum. Thus the universe and man's understanding of it unfolds dialectically. In short the universe with its consciousness—man—evolves."
>
> The result is that all possible particular positions are indeed relativized. While it is an oversimplification of Hegel's complete position, this has led to the idea that truth is to be sought in synthesis rather than antithesis. Instead of antithesis (that some things are true and their opposite untrue), truth and moral rightness will be found in the flow of history, a synthesis of them. . . . Today not only in philosophy but in politics, government, and individual morality, our generation sees solutions in terms of synthesis and not absolutes. When this happens, truth, as people had always thought of truth, has died.[7]

With truth no longer objective, and truth no longer an absolute but a synthesis of many sources, we can see the seedbed in which the historical-critical method of biblical interpretation flourished with Semler's view that not all of Scripture was the Word of God. Other voices came with theories and propositions. As was stated before, the floodgates were opened and God's Holy Word in Scripture was the target.

Hegel's use of opposing opposites against each other is called the dialectical method, later used by Karl Barth and other theologians committed to the historical-critical method of biblical interpretation. Reality was viewed, including the Holy Scriptures, as having no constancy and remained an open-ended option of interpretation because it had no fixed standards of right and wrong, no absolutes. With truth no longer objective and absolute, any critic theologian or philosopher had, and still has, carte blanche freedom to define his or her synthesis as truth.

Schleiermacher

A contemporary of Hegel was Friedrich Daniel Ernst Schleiermacher, who lived from 1763 to 1836. He has been named as the father of modern Protestant theology, but he should be grouped with Kant and Hegel. From these three scholars, liberal theology developed its structure, which was conducive to the legacy that the historical-critical method was to leave for future liberal theologians. A base for confusion and deception regarding Scripture as the Word of God was established.

Schleiermacher most definitely stands as a proponent of the historical-critical method, as he emphasized religious experience over God's revelation in Holy Scripture. Not only did he make religious experience the criterion of theology and the method of interpreting the Bible, but he maintained that the authority of Scripture can not stand as the foundation for faith.

Schleiermacher negated the power of the Scriptures to create faith through the power of the Holy Spirit. To him, only the New Testament had any relevance. He contended the Old Testament was included in the Bible only by virtue of its historical connection to the New Testament. His emphasis upon man and his religious experience trumped revelation from God in Scripture as having authority. Here once more is the subjective overriding the objective, man superior to God and His revelation in Holy Scripture.

Bengt Hagglund defined Schleiermacher's position regarding Christ's work:

> —or His suffering, death , and resurrection—has no bearing on salvation, but only His person, which represents the perfect consciousness of God. . . . Schleiermacher looked upon the Resurrection as resuscitation from apparent death, and he referred to the Ascension as Christ's actual death. Salvation refers only to "God being in Christ" (*das Sein Gottes in Christo*) and to the posthumous impact of His person—not to Christ's death and resurrection.[8]

James I. Packer, in describing the old liberalism *upon which the new liberalism is built,* (emphasis mine) wrote:

> In the first place, they accepted the viewpoint of the Romantic philosophy of religion set out by Schleiermacher—namely that the real subject-matter of theology is not divinely revealed truths, but human religious experiences. On this view, the proper study of theologians after all, is man. The Bible is a record of human action and reflection within which is embedded an experience of God, and our task is to dig that experience out. Scripture must be viewed, not as a divinely given record of a divinely given revelation, but as a by-product of the religious experience of the Hebrews; a record not so much of what God has said and done as of what some men thought He has said and done. The Bible is thus a memorial of the discovery of God by a nation with a flair

> for religion—that, and no more. The adoption of this approach was represented as a great advance. What it actually meant was that the pendulum had swung from the traditional habit of regarding Scripture only, or at least chiefly, as a divine book containing doctrinal truths to a new habit of regarding it only as a human book, a record of religious experiences.[9]

Even with this limited description of the development of the historical-critical method of biblical interpretation, the presuppositions of theologians stand out loud and clear. They stand as the foundation of the method and clearly define it. You, the lay person, can come to an understanding of the initial foundation, with more to come. The confusion and the deception mounts. Without a doubt, it is man standing as the judge, with the Holy Scriptures as the defendant.

One basic concept the historical-critical method maintains is the resistance of any and all presuppositions, which places authority before truth. The Bible no longer is the final and complete authority of truth. Instead, it must be the object of historical inquiry using science, psychology, sociology, secular literature, and the arts, as it searches for God's truth, believing God's truth can be revealed anywhere. Those disciplines became the multifaceted lens used to bring Scripture into proper focus. The focus it brought to you and to me, however, is the focus of post-modern relativism wherein truth has been emancipated from God and His Word. The word *truth* can be tied to any definition that man is capable of making. An avalanche of confusion and deception has been let loose upon us.

Kurt E. Marquart gave another insight into the development of the historical-critical method, which described the focus and intent of that method:

> . . . from the universities, where the clergy were trained, there spread upon the church a fearful mania of self-destruction—rationalistic unbelief. Since man has now 'come of age,' the external authority of divine revelation seemed embarrassing, if not insulting to his new dignity. Emancipated common sense was considered a fitting and sufficient guide also in matters of religion. The European intelligentsia, their heads turned by flattering visions of human grandeur and progress, were chaffing to break free from the hated authority of the Lord and of His Anointed: 'Let us free ourselves from Their rule, let us throw off Their control' (Psalm 2:3)! In an age of liberty, equality, and fraternity, it was unthinkable that one ancient book, the Bible, should retain any special privileges. Henceforth it was to be treated exactly like all other ancient documents. Stripped of its special, infallible status, the Bible was treated as just another ordinary citizen in the great republic of letters, all subject to the same laws and to the supreme court of critical scholarship. This and nothing else is the inner essence of the historical-critical method which originated at that time and was perfected in the nineteenth century.[10]

Notes

1. Gerhard Maier, *The End of the Historical-Critical Method,* (St. Louis: Concordia Publishing House, 1974), 15.
2. Van A. Harvey, op. cit., 39.
3. Alasdair I.C. Heron, *A Century of Protestant Theology,* (Philadelphia: The Westminster Press, 1980), .
4. Ibid., 2–21.
5. Martin Luther, *What Luther Says*, ed. Ewald M. Plass, 3 vol., (St. Louis: Concordia Publishing House, 1972), vol. III, 1355, #4368.

6. Carl E. Braaten, *Principles of Lutheran Theology,* (Philadelphia: Fortress Press, 1983), 40.

7. Francis A. Schaeffer, *How Should We Then Live?,* (Old Tappen, New Jersey: Fleming H. Revell Company, 1976), 162–163.

8. Bengt Hagglund, *History of Theology,* trans. Gene J. Lund, (St. Louis: Concordia Publishing House, 1966), 357.

9. James I. Packer, *Fundamentalism and the Word of God,* (Grand Rapids: William B. Eerdmans Publishing Company, 1983), 148.

10. Kurt E. Marquart, *Anatomy Of An Explosion,* (Grand Rapids: Baker Book House, 1977), 43.

Chapter 8

Questioning the Word of God—Strauss to Harnack

And now I commend you to God and to the word of His grace, which is able to build you up and to give you the inheritance among all those who are sanctified. (Acts 20:32)

In order to savor more of the flavor of confusion and deception that the historical-critical method has brought to God's Word in Scripture, a brief overview of some theologians of the nineteenth and twentieth centuries follows. The shift in the autonomy and authority of man over the Word of God, which began with the Enlightenment influence on Semler and Lessing, becomes more evident and clear in the emphases of these nineteenth and twentieth century scholars and theologians.

Strauss

David Freidrich Strauss (1808–1874) attacked the reliability of the Gospel accounts regarding Jesus. He maintained in his book, *Das Leben Jesus* (Life of Jesus), the

Gospel message in Matthew, Mark, Luke, and John was a myth, fashioned by the early Christian community. All the supernatural and messianic accounts in the Gospels were maintained to be myth because they could not be regarded as historical. Thus, Jesus was just an ordinary man, a teacher of morality and religion. Jesus was not the true God-man but symbolized humanity as a whole. Here is an example of the transcendence of God in Christ being reduced to immanence. The divinity of Jesus was attacked.

Harrisville and Sundberg commented on Strauss's view of Jesus when the historical truth of Scripture has been purged:

> To the question, "What of the historical now remained in the Jesus tradition?" Strauss gives the following answer: "Jesus grew up in Nazareth, permitted himself to be baptized by John, assembled disciples, went about teaching in the land of the Jews, everywhere opposed Pharisaism and invited people to the Messiah's kingdom, but in the end was subject to the hate and envy of the Pharisaic party, and died on a cross. This was the 'scaffold' that came to be festooned with the most varied and meaningful garlands of pious reflection and mythology."[1]

Harvey, in commenting on Strauss and the conflict between the biblical critic and authority, wrote:

> The issue was frequently clouded by the fact that the earliest Biblical critics sallied forth into speculative theology in the name of factual science. D.F. Strauss, for example, after a thousand or so pages of reasoned historical argument in his *Life of Jesus*, took pen in hand and charted a theological program for the future in which the doctrine of the Incarnation was to be supplanted by the idea of the deification of humanity.[2]

Baur

Strauss's former teacher, Ferdinand Christian Baur (1792–1860), took the presuppositions of Strauss to a more scientific level. Like Strauss, he questioned revelation, the Incarnation, and the bodily Resurrection of Jesus. He held that the historical reliability of Scripture was not accurate and did not have to be, because the important feature in Scripture was the theological idea.

Baur believed that in the early Christian church a rivalry existed between Peter and Paul. He saw Peter and those with whom he associated, as strict adherents to Jewish law, while Paul and his followers were proponents of a more liberal Greek approach, which did not emphasize Jewish law and ritual. This was the criteria for him to decide which books of the New Testament were authentic. Therefore, if a New Testament book didn't measure up to his standard, it was dismissed as a later production. For Baur, only four books written by Paul could pass his test: Romans, First and Second Corinthians, and Galatians. Baur also maintained the Gospels were deliberately invented. While Baur greatly influenced the development of the historical-critical method, he is considered to be more of a philosophical theologian than a biblical scholar.

Kierkegaard

Søren Kierkegaard, who lived from 1813 to 1855, a Danish philosopher as well as a lay theologian, is considered by many to be the originator of modern existential theology and of secular existentialism. This word *existentialism* may be a word that is unfamiliar to you. A definition from *Webster's Dictionary* is in order.

> *existentialism;* a chiefly 20th Century philosophical movement embracing diverse doctrines, but centering on analysis of individual existence in an unfathomable

> universe and the plight of the individual who must assume ultimate responsibility for his acts of free will without any certain knowledge of what is right or wrong or good or bad.[3]

With the above definition in mind, especially, "the individual must assume ultimate responsibility for his acts of free will without any certain knowledge of what is right or wrong or good or bad," the following is an interpretation of Kierkegaard's Christian existentialism given by Martin Heinecken, one of my professors at the Lutheran Theological Seminary at Philadelphia.

> Either the answer to man's need in his existence is met by his encounter with God in Christ, and here only, is "man" in his true being, or all this is an offense to man's autonomy. Either "every knee is to bow and every tongue confess that Jesus Christ is lord to the glory of the Father," or this is a presumptuous offense to the dignity of humanity. A man must make his choice.[4]

In Kierkegaard we see that man's reason only brings pessimism or despair, as he held that there was nothing within man's mind or reason that could produce any guarantee of absolute and unchanging truth. A problem for him was how the Bible could be the Word of God because he viewed it as only human words in which the presence of God was hidden. Reason could not extract it as truth. So God, to Kierkegaard, remained hidden, even in the Bible, until there was a surrender, an obedience-in-trust, a "leap of faith." This leap was over Lessing's "ugly ditch," discussed in the last chapter.

To Kierkegaard, when one is confronted by the living God in Christ, there can be only two responses: faith or offense. The former, the "leap of faith," was beyond reason.

It was man's choice to believe in the face of an objective uncertainty about Christ. In the face of that assertion, I must ask, "Where is the power of the Holy Spirit Who brings us to faith without a leap?" Holy Scripture is most clear when it maintains in the twelfth chapter of 1 Corinthians, verse 3: ". . .and no one can say, 'Jesus is Lord,' except by the Holy Spirit." The Holy Spirit makes faith a certainty! No "leap" is required.

Heinecken further stated:

> Kierkegaard contended that God is apprehended only in the inward passion of faith on the basis of an objective uncertainty. He repudiated all rationalistic fundamentalism which substitutes for objective uncertainty a supposedly infallible Bible. This was for him an evasion of the risk, the passion, the commitment, the obedience in which alone the living God is apprehended by an existing individual.[5]

At this point, it is important to see the difference between "objectivity" and "subjectivity." I asked several lay people to review what I had written, and along with their confusion over the word *existential,* they were also in the dark concerning the use of the words *objective* and *subjective,* as used in a theological or hermeneutical sense.

Objective truth, in the theological sense, is truth that can stand with firmness and certainty, because it comes from God as witnessed to in His Holy Word, the Scriptures. The God of creation is also the God of salvation in His Son, and the God of His body, the Church, which is empowered by His Holy Spirit, all *one* God. He empowered the writers of His Word to write with objective certainty His truth, His message.

It is propositional truth from God which is firm and does not waver. It is also verifiable truth, as many witnesses testify of God's mighty acts in both the Old and New Testaments. There is no myth in God's Word. God's truth in Holy Scripture validates itself by interpreting Holy Scripture *with* Holy Scripture, a subject that will be discussed later in Chapter 17. It stands as rock-solid objective truth from our Triune God. It is truth from God, independent of man.

Subjective truth, on the other hand, always involves man's interpretation of events or past writings, qualities, relationships, etc., which come forth as his mind's conclusions, as the subject of his experience or his investigation. It is man's reality expressed as truth. It is a Frank Sinatra singing: "I did it my way!"

In the theological or in the hermeneutical sense, it is man expressing himself and his views as truth in opposition to the objective, unwavering truth of God in Holy Scripture. Subjective truth is the Enlightenment position, in that it is the subject who defines reality or truth. Most of our colleges and universities are now structured to teach and do research according to subjective truth, a reality to which the person in the pew has little exposure or knowledge. The subjective landslide has already begun and has been with us for years wherein the historical-critical method of biblical interpretation has fastened on to that landslide and has "surfed" itself into theological prominence, a prominence that does not honor Scripture as the Word of God.

Why, then, are we so taken, influenced, as well as sickened, by opinion polls as they impact upon our lives? To a large degree, they reflect the subjective approach, "What is in it for me?" over and against an objective approach, "What is good for my community, church, nation and the world?" The answer lies in the conditioning of man to look to himself before he looks to God and His absolutes in Holy Scripture. The Scriptures have been so demeaned that they appear to be chaff blowing in the wind, without substance of truth. They appear on the scene as a cancerous tumor that must be eradicated, scholastically removed by liberal theologians. If they were not, mankind would have to submit to the authority of God over the scholastic, historical-critical ruminations of man. It is, in essence, the vaulting of subjectivity over the objectivity of the truth of God in His message in Scripture. It is man's "one-upmanship" over God wherein man must be the superior judge, and the Word of God the defendant.

The Bible, for Kierkegaard, was a word of the past, and only subjectivity, the leap of faith by the individual, is truth. He ruled out any truth in an objective certainty of the Bible. Yet, he did not discard the Bible but held it to be historical fact, within which the redemptive fact is hidden. He held that both historical and redemptive fact, constitute revelation but that there was no revelation without faith.

Subjectivity? Is this a return to the thinking of Kant? Almost so, as Kant held the will-to-truth higher than the will-to-believe. Kierkegaard upheld the will-to-believe in terms of "the leap of faith" as superior. Again, we see that in philosophy as well as in theology, the very basis for meaning has been separated or divorced from that which is objective, so that meaning has become the arena for the subjective interpretations of man.

No matter how you look at Kierkegaard, the Bible as the Word of God does not occupy top billing. To him, it was the subjective choice of faith by man that matters. In that existential moment before God, a moment that must be claimed again and again, faith must be claimed as a choice. It is all about subjectivity. Whatever is rational and logical in Holy Scripture, must be separated from faith, so that faith has no relationship to that which is rational and logical. God's written propositional communication to man in Scripture is way out in left field and only confuses the issue. As Heinecken maintained in his interpretation of Kierkegaard, it is better to trust the risen Lord and the Holy Spirit than the Holy Scriptures.[6]

While Kierkegaard did not use the so-called "tools" of the historical-critical method, what he did to the Word of God in Scripture accomplished a similar objective, in that its authority was questioned and challenged. For Kierkegaard, faith did not come from the working of the Holy Spirit, but as the result of a decision, a leap of faith, no matter how absurd that decision might appear. Thus Scripture, as the Word of God, was never regarded as the means by which God's Holy Spirit evoked faith.

Ritschl

The most important liberal theologian of the late nineteenth century was Albrecht Ritschl. He lived from 1822 to 1889. He was born in Berlin, Germany, and was the son of a bishop of the Prussian Protestant Church. His influence dominated liberal Protestantism in Germany so that the word "Ritschlianism" was equated with the liberal Protestantism of his time, and even beyond.

His theology evidenced a great concern for the actual and practical. He maintained that Christianity must be built on fact, so that we find God in history, where positive values come from Jesus, who then becomes the hero. Religion, then, is based on value judgments, and Jesus is indispensable, in that he has led mankind to discover the God of values. Ritschl redefined the work of Christ as being a moral example for mankind to follow.

Ritschl, and those who were his followers, abandoned metaphysics, the supernatural aspects of God in Christ, and centered theology in the historical Jesus and in the Jesus of faith, which man could find and relate to by means of value judgments. As such, Ritschl said or wrote very little about the Resurrection and Ascension of Jesus. Jesus, for Ritschl, had His impact on the world as a moral figure of integrity who continues to lead the community of the Kingdom of God.

Concerning this, Ritschl wrote:

> Christ made the universal moral Kingdom of God His end, and thus He came to know and decide for that kind of redemption, which He achieved through the maintenance of fidelity in His calling and of His blessed fellowship with God through suffering unto death. On the other hand, a correct spiritual interpretation of redemption and justification through Christ tends to keep more decisively to the front the truth that the Kingdom of God is the final end.[7]

A. Durwood Foster, in commenting on Ritschl, wrote:

> But for Ritschl the purpose which is revealed through the Bible and climactically in Christ is more than a soteriological one. (Soteriology is the doctrine of salvation. My notation here). As given in the notion of covenant and supremely in that of the kingdom of God, it aims at a universal community whose form is personal freedom and whose content is righteous love. Within the embracing goal of the kingdom, everyone has an individual moral vocation, which ideally includes the development of autonomous personality in dedicated service to the whole. Ritschl holds that only by being committed to the will of God in Christ—that is, to the good will for the whole—can true liberty be attained.[8]

Here, once more, we see what is done to Holy Scripture and its interpretation. A liberal view is applied, and the Jesus of Holy Scripture becomes a moral hero to build community in the Kingdom of God. Again, it is subjectivity over objectivity, one of the dread results of the historical-critical method. Scripture now becomes a mirror, or reflection, of man's historical experience and his self-interpretation, and is at his mercy. Any semblance of Scripture being the container of the timeless truths of God has been discarded. Scripture can no longer be trusted. It is the theologian or philosopher who is the authority and who instills trust by virtue of his experience and intelligent reason.

Harnack

Following in the footsteps of Ritschl was Adolf von Harnack who lived from 1851 to 1930. He was professor of history at the University of Berlin from 1888 until his retirement in 1921. He was accorded knighthood by Kaiser Wilhelm in 1914 and was a supporter of the Kaiser's plan for war. In fact, he was the author of the Kaiser's speech to the German people, in which he announced World War I. Ironically, one of his students was Karl Barth, who later rebelled against the liberalism of Harnack and those before him.

It was as an historian that Harnack viewed Scripture wherein he saw the heart of Christianity as the ethical righteousness of the Kingdom of God as taught by Jesus. As such, Harnack's theology flowed out of Ritschl. As one committed to the historical-critical method of biblical interpretation, he applied the method of the historian and felt free to pick and choose what he deemed worthy for his liberal theology. He gave little place to the Old Testament and regarded the accounts of angels and New Testament miracles as fantastic stories.

The crowning point of his theology is seen in the way he viewed Jesus, as he summoned theology away from the religion *about* Jesus to the religion *of* Jesus. Simply, he summed up his theology of Jesus in this way, revealing his flawed hermeneutics: "The Gospel, as Jesus proclaimed it, has to do with the Father only and not with the Son".[9]

Howard Clark Kee gave this assessment of Harnack:

> What Harnack did, therefore, in spite of his fully deserved reputation as one of the greatest historians of early Christianity and as a master of the literature of the church's early centuries, was to adopt a reductionist method of interpretation, by which he was able to brush aside those aspects of the gospel records that he found distasteful or (as he thought) unworthy of Jesus and thus arrive at a 'historical' core of the message of Jesus, a core that actually embodied the interpreter's own religious and ethical ideals. Despite Harnack's claim that he was interpreting the gospel accounts against the cultural and spiritual background in which Jesus actually lived, he selected those parts of the record that he found to be compatible with his own views and pronounced them to be authentic and historical. The principle of selection was not derived from the first-century documents but was imposed on them by early twentieth-century liberal humanitarianism.[10]

As the historian, Harnack, looked to internal experience, not biblical doctrine, as the essence for faith. His influence spread to the liberal American church scene of the early twentieth century, where the emphasis of preaching and teaching was "Life, not doctrine."

An optimism prevailed in liberal theology, so that it was man who was in control, man who could get a handle on the Christ and God of the Scriptures, because it was man, namely the historian, who could make the final definitions. The historian could then construct the gigantic hoop of hope through which man could gleefully jump on his way to life in a perfect Kingdom of God here on earth. The Jesus of Holy Scripture was abandoned. The Jesus of the historian's intellect was magnified as he used Jesus as putty in his hands, much like a sculptor molds and fashions his creation to fit the design and form he deems acceptable as fine art. A social gospel was embraced, devoid of the miraculous acts of God in Jesus. The values and ethics of the New Testament were in full bloom, while Jesus was placed in the shadows.

In the liberalism of the late nineteenth century, we see the historical-critical method of biblical interpretation alive and well, but did it feed the people of God? Was it a blessing? Was it an honor to God and His people?

Notes

1. Harrisville & Sundberg, op. cit., 99.
2. Van A. Harvey, op. cit., 6–7.
3. *Webster's Ninth Collegiate Dictionary* (Springfield, MA, Mermam-Webster Inc., 1986).
4. Martin J. Heinecken, *The Moment Before God,* (Philadelphia: Muhlenberg Press, 1956), 8.
5. Ibid., 259.
6. Ibid., 265.
7. Albrecht Ritschl, *The Christian Doctrine of Justification and Reconciliation,* trans. H. R. Mackintosh and A. B. Macaulay, (Edinburgh: T. & T. Clark, 1900), 10.
8. A. Durwood Foster and Albrecht Ritschl, *A Handbook of Christian Theologians,* eds. Dean. Peerman and Martin E. Marty, (Cleveland and New York: The World Publishing Company, 1965), 58–59.
9. Adolf von Harnack, *What Is Christianity?,* trans. T. B. Saunders, (New York: G. P. Putnam's Sons, 1901), 13.
10. Howard Clark Kee, *Jesus In History,* (New York: Harcourt Brace, & World, Inc., 1970), 16.

CHAPTER 9

Questioning the Word of God— Barth, Brunner, and Bultmann

Heaven and earth will pass away, but My words shall not pass away. (Matt. 24:35)

As the twentieth century began, the clouds of war turned into the torrent of death and destruction, which World War I unleashed upon Europe, with repercussions around the world. The liberal optimism of a world with man in firm control exploded and lay in ruins.

It was in this setting that a trio of theological giants emerged. Karl Barth, who lived from 1886 to 1968, Emil Brunner, who lived from 1889 to 1966, and Rudolf Bultmann, who lived from 1884 to 1976, were and are the hermeneutical giants of modern day theological seminaries, who have embraced the historical-critical method of biblical interpretation. Even seminaries committed to Holy Scripture as the Word of God, who are considered to be archaic, and "not with it," according to modern day hermeneutics, study this theological trio, along with other scholars who have given their biblical loyalty to that method of interpretation.

While the liberal optimism of the nineteenth century was rejected by these three theologians named above, the historical-critical method was embraced, but in a new way. Neo-orthodoxy was its name. Its primary view maintains that the Bible becomes the Word of God in a subjective sense, when God uses its testimony of witness to Jesus Christ to speak to people today. Neo-orthodoxy did not see the Bible as giving truth that can be stated in propositional language, which can be verified in history. As such, the Bible was also seen as void of moral absolutes.

Evangelical Dictionary of Theology gives this definition of neo-orthodoxy:

> Neo-orthodoxy is not a unified movement; it does not have a commonly articulated set of essentials. At best it can be described as an approach or attitude that began in a common environment but soon expressed itself in diverse ways. It began in the crisis associated with the disillusionment following World War I, with a rejection of Protestant scholasticism, and with a denial of the Protestant liberal movement which had stressed accommodation of Christianity to Western science and culture, the immanence of God, and the progressive improvement of mankind. . . . The movement was called neo-orthodox for a number of reasons. Some used the term in derision, claiming it had abandoned the traditional Protestant creedal formulations and was advocating a new "off" breed brand of orthodoxy. Others saw the movement as a narrowing of the traditional stance of Protestantism and thus to be avoided in favor of a more liberal stance. Those in sympathy with the movement saw in the word "orthodoxy" the effort to get back to the basic ideas of the Protestant Reformation

> and even the early church, as a means of proclaiming the truth of the gospel in the twentieth century; as in the prefix "neo" they saw the validity of new philological principles in helping to attain an accurate view of Scripture, which in turn and in combination with orthodoxy would provide a powerful witness to God's action in Christ for those of the new century.[1]

Barth

Karl Barth is considered to be the most influential theologian of the twentieth century and his theology can be described as dialectic—a term used in regard to Hegel in Chapter 7—a technique of opposing opposites against each other in the search for truth. Barth used the "yes" and "no" approach, for example, when he applied the "yes" to the truth of the transcendent Gospel of Jesus, but the "no" to the ability to justify an errorless biblical revelation in the Bible. It was in statement and counter-statement that God's truth could be expressed, so that God's truth was in constant dialectical activity. If it was stated that God is spoken of in His creation, then He must also be spoken of in His hiddenness, or concealment, in His creation.

He maintained that there are errors in Scripture because of the humanity of the writers, but that God still uses Scripture to proclaim His own Word of judgment, promise, and grace. Concerning the fallibility of Scripture he wrote,

> . . . the prophets and apostles as such, even in their office, even in their function as witnesses, were real, historical men as we are, and therefore sinful in their actions and capable and actually guilty of error in their spoken and written word.[2]

As such, the Bible can not be revelation, but a witness to the revelation of God. Therefore, the Bible functions as the Word of God by means of the witness of the prophets and apostles. In this witness, God causes it to be an event of proclamation. In the proclamation, man can be encountered with the Lordship of God. It becomes the Word of God in that function, the function of being an occasion for the Word of God to take place. Knowledge of God, therefore, becomes personal, subjective, not objective, not sure and certain. Here is seen the influence of Kierkegaard, which Barth acknowledged.

> . . . if I have a system, it is limited to a recognition of what Kierkegaard called "the infinite qualitative distinction" between time and eternity, and to my regarding this as possessing negative as well as positive significance: "God is in heaven, and thou art on earth." The relation between such a God and such a man, and the relation between such a man and such a God, is for me the theme of the Bible and the essence of philosophy.[3]

It is important to see that Barth had no use for the Bible as propositional truth from God, because the Bible does not have the authority of being the true Word of God as was maintained by Kierkegaard before Barth. Biblical authority can only reside in the true Word of God, Jesus, who comes as truth to encounter man in its proclamation.

Another way of stating this is to say that the Bible was given an instrumental use, rather than a propositional or authoritative use. Instrumental use in this sense means the Bible was just that—used as the means, the instrument to convey truth—rather than (being the *authority)* to convey the absolute truth of God. Propositional truth means truth that is knowable and can be believed. It can be believed because it is verifiable in the history of God's dealings with man. Its authority comes from God.

Barth's writings are voluminous, and this presentation and evaluation can only give a flavor of his hermeneutics, but it is obvious that his method of biblical interpretation lies within the framework of the historical-critical method. Yet, it must be noted that he along with Brunner and Bultmann, returned to theology the truth of the transcendence of God, which was a "right turn" from the liberal theology of the nineteenth century. However, it was not a turn to biblical orthodoxy wherein Scripture is believed as the inerrant and infallible Word of God.

James Barr, a proponent of the historical-critical method, gave the following understanding of Barth's position regarding the idea of the Word of God. This position is widely held today as a hermeneutical principle in many denominations.

> I shall outline the sort of general position, which would be recognized as Barthian. The average English speaker once again, if consulted about the meaning of terms, might say that "the Word of God" implies the same about the Bible as "inspiration" does; it would mean that the Bible comes from God, is the ultimate expression of his will, is without any kind of error. According to a more sophisticated current of theology, this is entirely wrong. God in his revealing reveals himself. He reveals himself in his Word, and that Word is Jesus Christ. In essence, therefore, and primarily, the Word of God is not the Bible; rather it is Jesus Christ himself; it is in him, according to St. John's Gospel, that the Word is incarnate. This does not mean that Jesus Christ, the Word of God, can be understood or approached apart from the Bible . . . the real revelatory content is not the Bible itself, but the person and acts to which it testifies. . . . It is wrong to say that the Bible is revelation; it

> is only witness to revelation . . . though the Word of God is not identical with the Bible, the Bible is an essential and appropriate access to the Word of God, and one cannot hope to hear the Word of God except through the mediation of the Bible. . . . The Word in the primary sense, Jesus Christ, speaks only as he is witnessed to by the scripture and proclaimed in faith by the church. The Bible is the Word of God only through its function of witness to God in his self-revelation; and it is the Word of God only as it is received in faith and proclaimed in the church.[4]

Since to Barth, the Bible is not revelation, he took the liberty in his interpretation of the Incarnation of Jesus Christ, the Virgin Birth, to assert that Jesus did not "become flesh" as John 1:14 declares, "And the Word became flesh, and dwelt among us, and we beheld His glory, glory as of the only begotten from the Father, full of grace and truth", but that Jesus assumed flesh. Barth wrote:

> As the Word of God becomes flesh He assumes or adopts or incorporates human being into unity with His divine being, so that this human being, as it comes into being, becomes as a human being the being of the Word of God.[5]

His Christology deviated dramatically from orthodox Christian Christology, regarding the Incarnation, which maintains that Jesus is one person, but declares that this person is the preexistent Son of God, who is the Second Person of the Trinity. He derives His eternal existence from God, and is therefore, God Himself. However, only as the Son is He who the Nicene Creed confesses, "who for us men and for our salvation came down from heaven and was incarnate by the Holy Ghost of the Virgin Mary, and was made man . . ." John in his Gospel declared, "And the

Word became flesh." Jesus as the Son of God is not changed in the Incarnation, so that he *assumes* flesh. He *became* flesh. He became a man for us and for our salvation.

Heinz Zahrnt commented on Barth's view of the Incarnation.

> Of the incarnation of God Barth seems to know nothing. He does not see God as genuinely entering history; the divine touches this world only "as a tangent touches a circle," "without touching it." The revelation of God is "a mathematical point" and consequently has "no secure standing place." It is not one historical event among other events of world history, but "the primal history," "non-historical happening," "time which is beyond time," "space which has no locality," "impossible possibility." It is not a light shining in the darkness, but lightning flashing in the night, or rather, lightning, which has already flashed. It is a "submarine island" which as soon as a clumsy foot attempts to walk upon it, is immediately covered once again by the all-concealing water. All in all, revelation conceals more than it manifests; it limits rather than reveals.[6]

When Barth disengaged, or separated, God's act of salvation in Jesus from the rest of Holy Scripture, what he did was crumble the truth of its objective foundation in the events through which it was revealed in Holy Scripture. By binding revelation exclusively to Jesus, Barth restricted knowledge about God the Father and God the Holy Spirit. Hans Urs von Balthasar described Barth's thought as an hourglass:

> . . . where God and man meet in the center through Jesus Christ. There is no other point of encounter between the top and bottom portions of the glass.[7]

The wedge, or divide, of Johann Salomo Semler between Holy Scripture and the Word of God can easily be seen in Karl Barth. While he employed the language of Holy Scripture, his system of theology is foreign to Holy Scripture. This is another example of confusion and deception.

Before Emil Brunner is discussed, another "time-out" from the constant flow of confusing words is in order. During this time-out, it might be helpful to provide a definition of an *existentialist.* An existentialist embraces diverse doctrines, but centers on analysis of individual existence in an unfathomable universe and must, therefore, assume ultimate responsibility for his acts of free will without any *certain* knowledge of what is right or wrong or good or bad.

Brunner

Emil Brunner was a contemporary of Barth, a lesser light than Barth, but nevertheless a theologian who was and is popular as a proponent of neo-orthodoxy. He and Barth both espoused the revelation of Jesus in Scripture as the primary and authentic revelation, but Brunner gave a different twist. He emphasized an "I-Thou" existentialist—personal—encounter in the human witness of the New Testament. The influence of Kierkegaard is again in evidence. The human "I" responds to the divine "Thou" in encounter. What happens in response determines the quality of life. Brunner adapted the "I-Thou" encounter from Martin Buber, a Jewish theologian.

He saw man being in revolt against such an encounter and saw Jesus enabling man to come to communion with God. This, he maintained, was the biblical view of truth, for it was from hearing the Word that the encounter takes place, and it is Jesus, Himself as the "Thou" meeting the "I." Brunner emphasized the place of the Christian community as the locus, or place, where the revelation through the biblical witness of the apostles primarily takes place. He wrote:

> The place of the Bible is primarily in the Christian community, not in the hands of the solitary believer. The public proclamation of the Word of Scripture, made necessary by the individual's imperfect understanding of the Scriptures, and, therefore, one which the mature Bible student can afford to ignore, but, just because it is public, connected with the community, it is the primary form of the Divine Revelation of the Word.[8]

Carl E. Braaten, in *Christian Dogmatics,* concerning the Virgin Birth of Jesus and how Brunner regarded it, wrote:

> In the Apostles' Creed we confess that Jesus was conceived by the Holy Spirit and born of the Virgin Mary. Since the Enlightenment, this has become one of the most disputed doctrines. In contemporary theology, Emil Brunner has denied the virgin birth of Christ in his book, The Mediator. He called it a "biological curiosity" and saw a possible connection with docetism because it made the Holy Spirit usurp the function of the human father. How could Jesus be like us in all respects if he did not actually have a human father? Karl Barth dismissed Brunner's arguments as "a bad business."[9]

To most Christians, *docetism* is an unfamiliar term. It is the name for the view that maintains that Christ did not have a real, but an apparent body, and therefore could not have suffered upon the cross. Any suffering was only imaginary. Obviously, this is heresy.

While Brunner detached what he called "the theory of the Virgin Birth" from the Incarnation, he did as Barth did, also claiming that Jesus *assumed* human nature. He downplayed any theorizing about Christ's nature in the Virgin Birth by claiming that the truth about Jesus is discovered through personal encounter with Him. Concerning the Resurrection, Brunner supported Barth, because it was the risen Lord to whom the apostles witnessed. This was for him the foundation for the proclamation of the encounter with Jesus.

In regard to the Old Testament and the Scriptures in general, he wrote:

> So far as the Scriptures of the Old Testament are concerned, the phrase "the Word of God" has far less final validity than in the New Testament. Here, indeed, the still greater variety and lack of unity of the teaching—and also of the narrative—warns us of the necessity for critical distinctions. . . . The less that the Scriptures are taken literally, the more room is there for the freedom of exposition—we might even say, for arbitrary interpretation; then every single exposition becomes a kind of Pope who alone possesses the right key to the meaning of the Scriptures. The Scriptures, then, become not a norm of doctrine, but a proof of a doctrine which stands independently of it; it is no longer a critical court of appeal, but is used merely to cover, or in any case to illustrate an interpretation of doctrine which is regarded as absolutely convincing.[10]

Brunner further stated concerning the Scriptures:

> . . . the Scriptures are the absolute authority, in so far as in them the revelation, Jesus Christ Himself, is supreme. But the doctrine of Scripture as such, although it is the

> absolute basis of our Christian doctrine, is only in a conditional sense the *norm* of the same. Critical reflection on the adequateness, or inadequateness, of the Biblical doctrinal testimony for the revelation to which it bears witness, is not eliminated; we still have to face it; a final resort to a single Scriptural passage is impossible for us. Hence, in each instance all Christian doctrine is, and remains, a virtue of faith.[11]

That Brunner was an advocate of the historical-critical method of biblical interpretation can not be denied. He had little use for Scripture that did not directly reveal an encounter with Jesus as an "I-Thou" encounter. Scripture could not stand as a norm or rule for doctrine. Thus, the Bible held little authority apart from the witness of the apostles to Jesus, which when proclaimed, was truth that he contended was not truth *about* Christ, but Christ Himself. As such, Christian doctrine could not be nailed down with any propositional truth that was knowable and believable by virtue of the fact that it came from the Word of God, which for confessional and orthodox Christians, is the basis for all doctrine. There was always the caveat or conditional clause for Scripture to be a norm for doctrine. If doctrine doesn't come from Scripture, from what source does it come?

Bultmann

Rudolf Bultmann was a New Testament scholar whose hermeneutical objective was to make faith in Jesus relevant and understandable to modern man. He believed that the New Testament was not concerned with the Jesus of history, only the Jesus of faith. Therefore, to insist on the historical accuracy of the Bible was to provide a support for faith that was illegitimate.

He used the Greek word, *kerygma,* to stand for the message of the early Christian church, the proclamation that was crucial for the decision of faith to occur. To find the essence of this *kerygmatic* proclamation for Bultmann was to disengage the proclamation from its New Testament form, which he called *myth.* He regarded the New Testament as having been written in mythical, miraculous thought forms, which were unintelligible to modern man. His only reliance was the *kerygma,* the preached and proclaimed message, the word of the Bible, a word that can not be proved to be the Word of God. He wasn't interested in the historical facts or background of the Bible, but only in proclamation of the message that produces an existential action, which is an encounter.

Bultmann maintained that the myth of the New Testament had to be demythologized—meaning it had to be translated, interpreted, or freed from the mythical language of the first century—into existential language. Then, modern man could be confronted and called to make a decision of faith, and thereby realize authentic existence. Here we see his thought relationship to Søren Kierkegaard. However, it was really Martin Heidegger who taught at the same time that Bultmann taught at the University of Marburg, Germany, who influenced him to use the existential motif.

The interpretation of the Bible for Bultmann depended on correct presuppositions, one of which he stated in this manner:

> Now, when we interpret the Bible, what is our interest? Certainly the Bible is an historical document and we must interpret the Bible by the methods of historical research. . . . But what is our true and real interest? Are we to read the Bible only as an historical document in order to reconstruct an epoch of past history for which the Bible serves as a "source"? Or is it more than a source?

> I think our interest is really to hear what the Bible has to say for our actual present, to hear what is truth about our life and about our soul.[12]

Another presupposition employed by Bultmann was the choice of philosophy over theology to provide the basis for the interpretation of the Bible. He wrote:

> Existentialist philosophy does not say to me "in such and such a way you must exist"; it says only "you must exist"; or since even this claim may be too large, it shows me what it means to exist . . . (Existentialism) is far from pretending that it secures for man a self-understanding of his own personal existence. For this self-understanding of my very personal existence can only be realized in the concrete moments of my "here" and "now." Existentialist philosophy, while it gives no answer to the question of my personal existence, makes personal existence my own personal responsibility, and by doing so it helps to make me open to the word of the Bible.[13]

To adopt Bultmann's existential view of the *kerygma* as proclamation apart from the historical and doctrinal foundation of Holy Scripture, presents a most narrow view of God; for then it is only as the proclamation of the message of Christ existentially encounters a person, that God in Christ and the person encountered, exist.

This is a reduction of God in Christ to an encounter with man. As such, the Virgin Birth, the life of Christ, the miracles He performed, His death and Resurrection and Ascension have no historical meaning apart from the existential encounter which takes place through the *kerygma*, the preaching, which of and in itself, becomes the revelation of God in which Christ meets man here and now in the faith encounter. Therefore, there can be no objective reality of Jesus as both Son of God and the human Jesus.

To Bultmann, the Bible was not the revelation of God, and in fact—Advent, Christmas, Good Friday, the Resurrection, the Ascension, and Pentecost, were seen as occurring on the same day, the day of proclamation. Bultmann has more than placed an existential meaning on the New Testament. He has cast aside the teachings of the New Testament.

Again, we see the confusion that follows when the historical-critical method is used so that the wedge of Semler, the wedge between the Word of God and Holy Scripture, was employed by Bultmann. For Bultmann, it was the proclamation of existential encounter that was magnified, while the Holy Scriptures and their historical and doctrinal content where confined to the shadows of myth.

The objective truth of God in Holy Scripture was once more abandoned or ignored for the primacy of a subjective existential encounter in which God and man play complementary roles. In sync with the historical-critical method, Bultmann tried to get behind the words of Scripture to emphasize the existential encounter in the *kerygma,* the proclamation.

Martin Warth critiqued Bultmann.

> In his intention to purify the message, Bultmann reduces it to the religious idea of encounter with God; but destroying the historical revelation of God by which He reveals and identifies Himself, Bultmann misses the most important of all: the correct identification of God.[14]

The trio of Barth, Brunner, and Bultmann have played and still do play important roles in hermeneutics today. Other theologians, such as Paul Tillich, will be discussed later, as they have laid the imprint of their hermeneutical interpretations on modern day and post-modern day theology. There is scarcely a seminary in which the historical-critical method is taught today that does not have a wide variety of devotees of those theologians in teaching positions of influence.

F. Forrester Church, a Unitarian minister, described his theological bond to Paul Tillich, and in so doing, gave a picture of the broad spectrum of Harvard Divinity School faculty members, devotees of theologians who were and are committed to the historical critical-method of biblical interpretation.

> . . . my first encounter with Paul Tillich was at Harvard, where he taught after leaving Union Theological Seminary and before going to the University of Chicago. By the time I entered Harvard, Tillich had been gone for more than a decade and was dead five years. Though I was assigned several of his books, no member of the faculty and no graduate student identified him- or herself to me as a "Tillichean." There were liberationist theologians of every possible stripe, and neo-Barthians, and Bultmanians, and disciples of Bonhoffer and Brunner. Many had been influenced by Tillich, but none professed allegiance to "the Tillich School."[15]

The bonding of theological students to theologians has been going on for centuries. Usually one finds such bonding occurring when impressionistic students suddenly find a theologian who either is championed by a professor they respect, or a theologian who mirrors their own presuppositions regarding the interpretation of Scripture.

In regard to this bonding, so impressive was the historical-critical method that dominated academic theological study in Germany by 1900 that it acted as a magnet in attracting students from other lands. Harrisville and Sundberg commented on this attraction.

> Protestant students flocked to Germany from abroad to learn the new liberal theology. They carried back to their homelands the message and the techniques of historical criticism, eagerly adapting them to needs of progressive cultural factions within their own denominations and societies. Through trials and tribulations, wars and cultural changes, this liberal theology has been tenacious in its hold on the imagination of biblical scholars. It has been eminently successful in the fulfillment of its original mandate. For significant portions of the Christian intellectual elite in the West, Christianity has been made to conform to the tenants of the Enlightenment world view.[16]

My son, Eric, is the pastor at Christ Lutheran Church, an LCMS congregation in Coos Bay, Oregon. He tells the story of a woman student at the Lutheran Theological Seminary at Berkeley, California— an ELCA seminary—and how conformity to the "tenants of the Enlightenment world view" took its hold on her. One evening while he was studying, the stillness that permeated his dormitory area was suddenly shattered by a female voice shrieking in the hall outside his room, "I know who I am! I know who I am! I'm a Barthian Lutheran! I'm a Barthian Lutheran!"

Yes, theologians do have "theological sheep," and the trio of Barth, Brunner, and Bultmann have had, and still do have, quite a following, not only among seminarians, but also among ordained pastors and professors who have adopted as their own, the historical-critical views of their mentors. Confusion is contagious. Deception knows no bounds. The people of God who are subjected to such confusion and deception are the innocent victims.

Notes

1. Walter A. Elwell, ed., op. cit., 754–755.
2. Karl Barth, *Church Dogmatics,* eds., G.W. Bromiley and T.T. Torrance, (New York: Charles Scribners Sons, 1961), I,2, 528–529.
3. Karl Barth, *The Epistle To The Romans,* trans. Edwyn C. Hoskyns, (London: Oxford University Press, 1933), 10.
4. James Barr, op. cit., 18–19.
5. Karl Barth, *Church Dogmatics,* I,2, 160.
6. Heinz Zahrnt, *The Question of God,* trans. R. A. Wilson, (New York: Harcourt Brace & World, Inc., 1961), 28.
7. Hans Urs von Balthasar, *The Theology of Karl Barth,* trans. John Drury, (New York, Chicago, San Francisco: Holt, Rinehart and Winston, 1976), 170.
8. Emil Brunner, *The Divine Imperative,* trans. Olive Wyon, (Philadelphia: Westminster Press, 1947), 312–313.
9. Carl E. Braaten, *Christian Dogmatics,* eds. Carl E. Braaten and Robert W. Jensen, (Philadelphia: Fortress Press, 1984), vol.1, 546.
10. Emil Brunner, *The Christian Doctrine of God,* trans. Olive Wyon, (Philadelphia: Westminster Press, 1949), 47–48.
11. Ibid., 49.
12. Rudolf Bultmann, *Jesus Christ and Mythology,* (New York: Charles Scribners Sons, 1958), 51–52.
13. Ibid., 55–56.
14. Martin Warth, *"Theologies" in Evangelical Directions For The Lutheran Church,* eds. Erich Kiehl and Waldo J. Werning, (Chicago, 1970), 18.
15. *Paul Tillich, The Essential Tillich,* ed. F. Forrester Church, (New York: Macmillan Publishing Company, 1987), xv.
16. Harrisville & Sundberg, op. cit., 267.

Chapter 10

Questioning the Word of God–Tillich

The grass withers, the flower fades, But the word of our God stands forever. (Isa. 40:8)

Tillich

Of all the theologians considered so far (and they are by no means exhaustive of those who were committed to the historical-critical method of biblical interpretation), Paul Tillich stands out as the most difficult to understand, because of his philosophy of religious language. Tillich has been regarded as the father of radical theology, which evolved in the mid-1960s, as he set the tone for radical thought about God. He lived from 1886 to 1965. He was born in Starzeddel in Prussia and was the son of a Lutheran pastor. Following his father's footsteps, he was ordained as a Lutheran pastor in 1912.

During World War I, he served as a chaplain in the German Armed Forces where the trauma of battle had far reaching consequences for Tillich. He suffered two nervous breakdowns, which could have caused a crisis of doubt that had an influence on his view of God.

His great concern was to inner-connect theology, philosophy, religion, and culture. In his later years, he sought to relate Christianity to other religions, especially the eastern religions. He held that philosophy asks the questions concerning the existence of life and that theology answers them.

As such, philosophy was the platform from which to launch theology. The form of philosophy that Tillich emphasized is known as *ontology*. Ontology is the study of being.

Regarding this he wrote:

> Philosophy asks the question of reality as a whole; it asks the question of the structure of being. And it answers in terms of categories, structural laws, and universal concepts. It must answer in ontological terms. Ontology is not a speculative-fantastic attempt to establish a world behind the world; it is an analysis of those structures of being which we encounter in every meeting with reality. . . . Philosophy necessarily asks the question of reality as a whole, the question of the structure of being. Theology necessarily asks the same question, for that which concerns us ultimately must belong to reality as a whole; it must belong to being. Otherwise we could not encounter it, and it could not concern us. Of course, it cannot be one being among others; then it would not concern us infinitely. It must be the ground of our being, that which determines our being, or not-being, the ultimate and unconditional power of being. . . . Philosophy and theology ask the question of being. But they ask it from different perspectives. Philosophy deals with the structure of being in itself; theology deals with the meaning of being for us. From this difference convergent and divergent trends emerge in the relation of theology and philosophy.[1]

The above quote is given as an example of the way Tillich looked at theology, and if there were any biblical references, it would be purely coincidental. Philosophy held more emphasis in his theological method than Holy Scripture. As a proponent of the historical-critical method, in that he stood as a judge upon Holy Scripture, one has only to look at his definition of "Word of God" to understand his scriptural orientation.

He gave six different meanings to the term "Word of God." First, it is "the divine manifestation in the ground of being itself." Second, it is "the medium of creation." Third, it is "the manifestation of the divine life in the history of revelation." Fourth, it is "the manifestation of the divine life in the final revelation. The Word is a name for Jesus as the Christ . . . the being of Christ, of which his words and his deeds are an expression." Fifth,

> The term Word is applied to the document of the final revelation and its special preparation, namely, the Bible. But if the Bible is called the Word of God, theological confusion is almost unavoidable. Such consequences as the dictation theory of inspiration, dishonesty in dealing with the biblical text, a "monophysitic" dogma of the infallibility of a book, etc., follow from such an identification. The Bible is the Word of God in two senses. It is the document of the final revelation; and it *participates* (emphasis mine) in the final revelation of which it is the document. Probably nothing has contributed more to the misinterpretation of the biblical doctrine of the Word than the identification of the Word with the Bible.[2]

Sixth, "the message of the church as proclaimed in her preaching and teaching is called the Word."

When Tillich used the word *participate* in the previous quote, he was indicating he could not find a major role for the Bible in revelation. Therefore, nothing from the Bible, and even the historical reality of Jesus, could be regarded as absolute truth.

In place of God's Word, stood "being itself," or what he referred to as "the ground of being," as having any relevance for ultimate concern. Tillich's view of revelation in regard to the Word of God can be understood in the following illustration he gave:

> No minister should claim more than his intention to speak the Word when he preaches. He never should claim that he has spoken it or that he will be able to speak it in the future, for, since he has no power over the revelatory constellation, he possesses no power to preach the Word. He may speak mere words, theologically correct though they may be. And he may speak the Word, though his formulations are theologically incorrect. Finally, the mediator of revelation may not be a preacher or religious teacher at all but simply someone whom we meet and whose words become the Word for us in a special constellation.[3]

Revelation apart from the Word of God, whether casual human words or natural revelation, was very much a part of Tillich's theology.

Words fly with Tillich! One, which he used as a vehicle of theological flight, is the word *correlation*. He defined it this way: "The method of correlation explains the contents of the Christian faith through existential questions and theological answers in mutual interdependence."[4] In his use of correlation, the whole world of academic thought, as well as existential experience, is invited to the table upon which lies the "content of the Christian faith" as he defined it in his theology according to the ontological ground rules of "being"—certainly not according to biblical revelation in Holy Scripture. Correlation, as in synthesis, like a mixing of ingredients in a meat loaf before it is molded and baked, stands as the theological solution. Questions and answers—questions and answers—the questions raised by philosophy or other ideologies, and the answers given by a theology that has no connection to a historical Jesus or a God revealed in Holy Scripture, are but a mishmash of separate ingredients—unpalatable, unfinished.

His relationship to existentialism was integral to his theology. He wrote:

> The systematic theologian . . . needs the help of creative representatives of existentialism in all realms of culture. He needs the support of the practical explorers of man's predicament, such as ministers, educators, psychoanalysts, and counselors. The theologian must reinterpret the traditional religious symbols and theological concepts in the light of the material he receives from these people. He must be aware of the fact that terms like 'sin' and 'judgment' have lost not their truth but rather an expressive power which can be regained only if they are filled with the insights into human nature which existentialism (including depth psychology) has given to us . . ."[5]

". . .creative representatives of existentialism in all realms of culture"? Are these the authorities upon which theology is built? That the existentialism of Kierkegaard was alive and well in Tillich can not be denied. Here again it is many voices speaking. Can deception and confusion stand in more clear light?

Words that Tillich wrote have become implanted in modern day theology as "truth." One set of words that really have had an impact are, "The Bible does not contain words of God . . . but it can and in a unique way, has become the 'Word of God.'" The more complete quote stated:

> The Bible does not contain words of God (or as Calvin has said, divine "oracles"), but it can and in a unique way has become the "Word of God." Its uniqueness resides in the fact that it is the document of the central revelation, with respect to both its giving and receiving sides. Every day, by its impact on people inside and outside the church, the Bible proves that it is the Spirit's most important medium in the Western tradition. But it is not the only medium, nor is everything in it always such a medium. In many of its parts it is always a potential medium, but it only becomes an actual medium to the degree that it grasps the spirit of men."[6]

Duane A. Priebe, a theologian at Wartburg Theological Seminary, Dubuque, Iowa—a seminary now a part of the ELCA—picked up on the above theme from Tillich when he wrote, "We listen for a Word from God in which the text that once was God's Word to people in a different time and place might again become God's Word for us."[7] That this is a constant position and theme of those committed to the historical-critical method can not be denied.

Tillich did a lot of revising of biblical terms and concepts. He called God "the ground of being" or "being itself" or the "God above God." Jesus was termed as "the New Being, the Christ."

One concept or doctrine that he felt needed revision was the Incarnation. He wrote:

> Who is the subject of Incarnation? If the answer is "God," one often continues by saying that "God has become man" and that this is a paradox of the Christian message.

> But the assertion that "God has become man" is not paradoxical but a nonsensical statement.[8]

Tillich believed the Incarnation needed to be reinterpreted to have the meaning that Jesus was "essential man appearing in a personal life under the conditions of existential estrangement."[9] As such, Jesus was not considered by Tillich to be divine or to have a divine nature. Instead, he brought out through his humanity an entirely new order of being, so that the original order of God and humanity was restored; this restoration stood as his Christhood, the New Being. The orthodox Christian doctrine that Jesus is both true God and true man was abandoned by this theologian.

Grenz and Olson, in critiquing Tillich, stated:

> . . . his phrase "God above God" became a more literal description of his doctrine than he intended. But which "God" was Tillich's God? Was it the absolute God, "Being itself," untouched by existence, or was it the God intrinsically involved in the process of the world with all its conflicts and tensions? . . . the overall cast of his theology favors the latter. It leans heavily toward pantheism and thus, in the final analysis must be judged to be a case of radical immanentism. This explains why certain proponents of "Christian atheism" in the 1960s proclaimed him as their mentor.[10]

Immanentism is defined by Webster as "any of several theories according to which God or an abstract mind or spirit pervades the world." Has Tillich been true to Holy Scripture as the Word of God? Would he have been a good Sunday School teacher for our youth? The answer is found in your presupposition concerning the Word of God. Is Holy Scripture really the Word of God, or have we been deceived? Better questions are: Who is doing the deceiving, God or man? And: Are the critics who use the historical-critical method rendering honor and blessing to God or to the deceiver of Adam and Eve?

Radical theologians like Bishop John A. T. Robinson, the Anglican Bishop of Woolwich, England, looked to Tillich as their mentor. Their intent was to save theology and make it understandable in a secular culture. They attempted to do away with the transcendence of God as they emphasized His immanence. They didn't see God as "up there" or "out there," because to them God as transcendent was dead; while God as immanent, God within the ground of being, was alive and well.

In the 1960s, this fermented into the "Death of God" movement, which called into question many of the basic assumptions and doctrines held by Christians for centuries. Another theologian who championed secular theology about God was Paul van Buren. Following his death in 1998, *The Christian Century* commented on his passing and some of his work.

> In his noted 1963 book *The Secular Meaning of the Gospel: Based on an Analysis of its Language,* which established his reputation as a nontraditional theologian, van Buren argued that he was "trying to find an utterly nontranscendent way of interpreting the gospel" so "sense could be made of it." Some theologians critical of van Buren's methodology and thinking countered that if faith is stripped of transcendence, there is little left of religion.[11]

Bishop Robinson in his book, *Honest to God,* leans heavily on Tillich in trying to establish immanence over transcendence, as he quoted various portions of his sermon, *The Depth of Existence.* "It opened my eyes to the transformation that seemed to come over so much of the traditional religious symbolism when it was transposed from the heights to the depths." He then quoted Tillich:

> The name of this infinite and inexhaustible depth and ground of all being is *God.* That depth is what the word *God* means. And if that word has not much meaning for you, translate it, and speak of the depths of your life, of the source of your being, of your ultimate concern, of what you take seriously without any reservation. Perhaps, in order to do so, you must forget everything traditional that you have learned about God, perhaps even the word itself. For if you know that God means depth, you know much about him. You cannot think or say: Life has no depth! Life is shallow. Being itself is surface only. If you could say this in complete seriousness, you would be an atheist; but otherwise you are not. He who knows about depth knows about God.[12]

Francis Schaeffer gave this insight into Tillich and his theology:

> Paul Tillich (1886–1965) of Harvard Divinity School was one of the outstanding neo-orthodox theologians. A student related to me that when Tillich was asked just before his death in Santa Barbara, California, "Sir, do you pray?" he answered, "No, but I meditate." He was left only with the word *God*, with no certainty that there was anything more than just the word or that word equaled anything more than the pantheistic pan-everythingism. The God-is dead theology which followed Tillich concluded logically that if we are left only with the word *God*, there is no reason not to cross out the word itself.[13]

John Warwick Montgomery offered this critique of Tillich:

> Tillich, like other major theologians of the 20th century, uncritically accepted Lessings claim that eternal truth cannot be accepted with historical revelation and likewise bought the negative biblical criticism of the 19th century. Thus, he eliminated the possibility of his making concrete and verifiable statements about God or about His relation to the world.[14]

The circus of the historical-critical method continued with Tillich, but did not end with him. Others followed and performed to the glory of man's intelligence, not to God's revealed truth in His Holy Word. A common thread of commitment to the historical-critical method was and still is the arrogance of sinful man to assume that he or she knows more about revelation than our God who reveals His truth in His Holy Word and in His Son, Jesus.

Theologians committed to the historical-critical method agree that revelation has, as its object, God—His person—but not propositional truth about God, which can be substantiated and cross-referenced by the revelation of God in Holy Scripture, so that Holy Scripture is its own interpreter. Thus, they are free of Scripture as the Word of God and they can present their "theologies" about a person. They redefine that person according to their system, so that the one doing the defining is the authority and not the Holy Scriptures, which come from our all powerful, all-present, and all knowing God: Father, Son, and Holy Spirit. Paul Tillich stands out as such a theologian when he wrote:

> There are no revealed doctrines, but there are revelatory events and situations which can be described in doctrinal terms . . . the "Word of God" contains neither revealed

> commandments nor revealed doctrine. It accompanies and interprets revelatory situations.[15]

No wonder Tillich could reinterpret the Crucifixion and the Resurrection of Jesus. It is also most interesting to note that in his systematic theology, Tillich never allowed the Bible to speak for itself. It was muted. Regarding the Crucifixion and the Resurrection he wrote:

> . . . one can say that the historical event underlying the Crucifixion story shines with comparative clarity through the different and often contradictory legendary reports. Those who regard the passion story as cult-legend, which is told in various ways, simply agree with the thesis presented about the symbolic character of the Cross of the Jesus who is the Christ. The only factual element in it having the immediate certainty of faith is the surrender of him who is called the Christ to the ultimate consequence of existence, namely, death under the conditions of estrangement. Everything else is a matter of historical probability, elaborated out of legendary interpretation.
>
> The event which underlies the symbol of the Resurrection must be treated in an analogous way. The factual element is a necessary implication of the symbol of the Resurrection (as it is of the symbol of the Cross). Historical research is justified in trying to elaborate this factual element on the basis of the legendary and mythological material which surrounds it. But historical research can never give more than a probable answer. The faith in the Resurrection of the Christ is neither positively nor negatively dependent upon it. Faith can give certainty only to the victory of the Christ over the ultimate consequence of the existential estrangement to which he subjected himself. And faith can give this

> certainty because it is itself based on it. Faith is based on the experience of being grasped by the power of the New Being through which the destructive consequences of estrangement are conquered.[16]

Now, preacher, make *that* the center of your Good Friday and Easter sermons!

Now, lay person in the pew, do you understand, or are you confused? It seems that a Chinese writer of over 2300 years ago by the name of Sun Tzu, quoted as this book began, is correct and most relevant in today's theological world where confusion and deception reigns. "All warfare is based on deception."

You, who sit in the pews Sunday after Sunday and long for the pure and sweet message of God's Word, are you filled with God's Word, preached as the inerrant and infallible Word that comes from Holy Scripture? Or are you led to believe that theologians, committed to and embracing the historical-critical method of biblical interpretation, have a more relevant and meaningful answer to your spiritual needs? It can not be both ways. You, as well as the unchurched person on the street, can be caught in the midst of this controversy of deception and confusion.

As a Navy chaplain, while still endorsed by the LCA—now the ELCA—my wife, Barbe, and I always joined an LCA congregation in the area where we were stationed. In that association we were in contact with church members who were mystified and confused by new interpretations given to Holy Scripture where the Bible was questioned as the Word of God, and were told that it "only contained the Word of God and was not throughout, the Word of God."

In one congregation where we were members (because of the nature of my chaplaincy duties when not in a travel status) I was able to teach a Bible class in a congregational setting where I maintained that Scripture was the Word of

God. The attendance increased by leaps and bounds, and we had to find larger quarters, as the lay people were hungry for the objective and propositional Word of God in Holy Scripture over the subjective musings of pastors committed to the historical-critical method. Yes, God's inerrant and infallible Word does have power for God's people!

So far we have seen paramount in the preceding theologies, the subjectivity of biblical interpretation, where man stands as the judge over the objective Word of God. That subjectivity ranges from Hegel, where truth was no longer objective, but a synthesis of many sources. . . .

To Schleirmacher, whose view that religious experience became the criterion of theology and the method of interpreting the Bible. . . .

To Strauss, where all the supernatural and messianic accounts in the Gospels were myths, because they could not be regarded as historical. . . .

To Kierkegaard, where the Bible was a word of the past and only subjectivity—"the leap of faith" by the individual—is truth. . . .

To Ritschl, who regarded Jesus only as a moral figure, a hero, an example to follow. . . .

To Harnack, who viewed Scripture wherein he saw the heart of Christianity as the ethical righteousness of the Kingdom of God as taught by Jesus. . . .

To Barth, who had no use for the Bible as propositional truth, but only for the proclamation of the acts of Jesus to which it testified. . . .

To Brunner, who maintained the "I-Thou" existential encounter within the Christian community where the revelation through the biblical witness of the apostles primarily takes place; and his position that the less the Scriptures are taken literally, the more room there is for the freedom of exposition—we might even say, for arbitrary interpretation; then every single exposition becomes a kind of pope who alone possesses the right key to the meaning of the Scriptures. . . .

To Bultmann, whose use of the word *kerygma* as the message and proclamation of the early church—a proclamation that had to be disengaged from the myth of its New Testament form by demythologizing, interpreting the language of the first century into existential language, so that man could be confronted in his existence and make a decision of faith, and thus realize his authentic existence. . . .

To Tillich and his ontology of "being itself" wherein the Bible does not contain words of God, but can become, in a unique way, the Word of God, in which the theologian needs "the help of creative representatives of existentialism in all realms of culture."

The above curt summary is cut out of a single bolt of cloth—the historical-critical method of biblical interpretation. In this light, Richard J. Coleman has given the following insight regarding the subjectivity of man and how that subjectivity brings confusion and uncertainty to the Word of God:

> Whenever subjective and relative standards are allowed to speak for God, the inevitable outcome is confusion and uncertainty about what constitutes the Word of God. If Scripture is not its own authority, and if Scripture does not testify to its own authority and interpret itself, than there is no other choice but to look for other relative authorities which can stand alongside the relative authority of God's written word. And this, says the evangelical, is precisely what we find within liberalism. The authority of Scripture becomes dependent upon other authorities—for example, the results of historical criticism, the interpretive role of the church and oral tradition, human reason and experience. We find a multiplicity of hermeneutical principles jockeying for

> acceptance as the correct method to interpret Scripture. We find the individual free to choose his own method of interpretation, his own philosophical presuppositions, his own rule of thumb to distinguish between historical fact and fable. We find that liberals have lost confidence in the Bible: it is seldom read, generally referred to as a norm among other norms, and conspicuously absent from the church's preaching.[17]

Once more we come upon the theme of many voices speaking so that confusion is rampant. Which critic or theologian has the magic key to unlock Holy Scripture and lay the gem of the Word of God before us? This question is at the heart of the matter, for it seems all the critics disagree with each other as they postulate their individual theories and conclusions. Diversity and pluralism run rampant among those who espouse the historical-critical method. It is a hodgepodge or jumble of confusion that plagues the Christian church today. The consequences of this historical-critical method upon the people of God will be considered later in Chapter 13.

Notes

1. Paul Tillich, *Systematic Theology,* (Chicago: The University of Chicago Press, 1967), I, 20–22.
2. Ibid., I, 157–159.
3. Ibid., I, 159.
4. Ibid., I, 60.
5. Ibid., II, 28.
6. Ibid., III, 124–125.
7. Duane A. Priebe, *Studies in Lutheran Hermeneutics,* eds. John Reumann, Samuel H. Nafzger, and Harold H. Ditmanson, (Philadelphia: Fortress Press, 1979), 296.
8. Paul Tillich, op. cit., I, 94.

9. Ibid., I, 95.

10. Stanley J. Grenz and Roger E. Olson, *20th Century Theology,* (Downes Grove, Illinois: InterVarsity Press, 1992), 130.

11. *The Christian Century,* (15–22 July l998), 675.

12. John A. T. Robinson, *Honest To God,* (Philadelphia: The Westminster Press, 1963), 21–22.

13. Francis A. Schaeffer, *How Then Should We Live?,* (Old Tappan, New Jersey: Fleming H. Revell Company, 1976), 178.

14. John Warwick Montgomery, *The Suicide of Christian Theology,* (Minneapolis: Bethany Fellowship Inc., 1970), 32.

15. Paul Tillich, op. cit., I, 125.

16. Ibid., II, 154–155.

17. Richard J. Coleman, *Issues Of Theological Conflict,* (Grand Rapids: William B. Eerdmans Publishing Company, 1971), 174–175.

Chapter 11

Questioning the Word of God—Some Modern Attempts

So faith comes from hearing, and hearing by the word of Christ. (Rom. 10:17)

Process Theology

In universities and seminaries, a newfound theology, or philosophy, has gained interest and attention. It is called Process theology, in which God and man are co-creators in a secular theology. Process theology holds that reality is determined by becoming, an on-going process, rather than a static state of being. It brings God, the world of nature, and human beings and their shared experience, together, so that they influence one another in a temporal, a *now* process, that goes on and on and on . . . *ad infinitum.*

In this theology, God does not stand as the Creator of the world, who created the world *ex nihilo* (out of nothing) as Holy Scripture attests, but as a co-creator, a co-participator in the process of becoming. In this process, God is ever-changing, not permanent or fixed, because anything that is static or fixed is viewed as being evil, and since God is not viewed as evil, He, too, must also be in the process of becoming. God as transcendent is ignored, while God as immanent in the process is emphasized.

The early pioneers of this philosophy were Alfred North Whitehead and Charles Hartshorne. The Divinity School of the University of Chicago has been one of the centers that have championed this philosophy as theology.

In regard to Jesus being God Incarnate, meaning Jesus as God in human flesh, Process theologians take another view. They see Jesus, not as God, but as an ethical human being, who was more intimately connected and open to God's teachings than other humans, and as such, is a model or an example of how to love God and mankind. Griffen and Cobb pointed out that Jesus, more than any other human being:

> was himself open to creative transformation. Therefore, insofar as we genuinely receive Jesus as the revelation of the basic truth about reality, we are more open to the divine impulses in our experience and accordingly, are more apt to respond positively to (them).[1]

Because Process theology is entangled in metaphysics, a division of philosophy that deals with the fundamental nature of reality and being, it wed itself to science as it emphasized the importance of the sciences in theological formation. There are many philosophers and theologians who have connected themselves to this theology, and as can be expected, there are many disagreements among them.

A meaningful approach to partially understanding this theology/philosophy, is through their view of Holy Scripture. Regarding this, David Basinger has written:

> For many conservative Christians in the classic tradition, the Scriptures are not simply a collection of the best thoughts of humans. They are in some sense the inspired words of God, which are, as such, capable of giving us valuable information that could not be acquired through human effort alone. Process theists, of course, cannot accept a literal interpretation of this model of inspiration. They grant that the writers of Scripture may have been more attuned to God than we are and, thus, that some (or much) of what we read in the Bible might enable us to better open ourselves up to how God would have us think and act. But they must deny that the origin of Scripture breaks the metaphysical mold. All the writers of Scripture were—as we are—individuals who at every moment encountered a past, considered the real options for future activity offered by God and the world and then made a choice. Thus there is no basis for maintaining that what we find in the Scriptures is some sort of special, direct revelation from God. And although the Scriptures are seen as significant, most process theists see no reason why the thoughts of others, past and present, cannot have equal spiritual value.[2]

From the above, it is plain to see that Process theologians have no use for the absolutes of God as revealed in Holy Scripture, because they contend that God is not the author of His Word. Their philosophy accommodates the relativity of man's penchant or inclination to be his own "god" wherein he or she can equate their goals and actions as being on the level of divine action as they stand as co-creators with God in the indefinable process of "becoming." Sinful man and his thoughts can now rise as *equal* to God's thoughts or to anything the Bible proclaims.

In reviewing John B Cobb's book, *GOD and the WORLD,* I looked in vain for one, just one quote from Scripture to which he would make reference regarding Process theology, or rather, philosophy. He quoted theologians, evolutionists, a behavioral scientist, but never the Scriptures. Yes, there did appear one reference to Scripture, but that was from Dietrich Bonhoeffer who referred to Matthew 8:17 and was quoted by Cobb. His reason for a person being a Christian reveals his philosophical orientation and the orientation of process thinkers in general.

> The reason for being a Christian is *not* that one necessarily is or ought to be religious and that Christianity is the best religion. The argument must be rather that Christianity is truer to reality and/or that it more adequately illumines and fulfills man's ultimate needs, both as an individual and social being.[3]

Basinger gives us another opportunity to view the process procedure of regarding God. Certainly, the Trinity has been ruled out along with Jesus as God's Incarnate Son dying on the cross for our sins and rising triumphantly as our Risen Lord on Easter, the conqueror of sin and death.

Basinger wrote:

> Finally, to cite one last example, many classical Christians have thought it important to hold that God is omniscient in the sense that all that has occurred, is occurring or will occur (including what we will freely choose to do) is open to the divine vision. But process theists,

> not surprisingly, deny that God possesses such insight. God does, they acknowledge, know all that has occurred. However, since all reality is co-creative—since every droplet of experience includes the self-determination of entities other than God—God cannot know in advance what the choices of any entity will be. God can, of course, accurately predict what will occur to a greater degree than we. But no certain knowledge of the future is possible even for God, it is argued, for there is presently nothing certain about the future for God to know.[4]

It has been stated by those committed to this process that they feel a warmth and contentment for a deity who stands by their side and feels the pain as well as the joys of life as they face life's struggles. The real tragedy, of course, is the abandonment of our God: Father, Son, and Holy Spirit, and the revelation of His Word in Scripture from which we draw the doctrines we confess as God's truth for all of life. And then, God has no certainty about tomorrow. He is just a "feeble" God.

Add to that, the living presence of Jesus in the hearts and lives of His people as Lord, not just an example, and you can see what Process theology/philosophy has passed by. In regard to Process philosophy, if we would ask, "Who is in control?" those who embrace this philosophy would have to respond, "We are!" Other questions that can be asked are: Is this theology or philosophy Christian? Can the word *Christian* even be associated with a theology or philosophy where Jesus is not regarded as Son of God or Savior—but a human being who is also in the process?

Could this theology or philosophy have ever come to such a place of prominence in the theological world of our universities and seminaries without the historical-critical method? Maybe it could have, but when the historical-critical method is understood for what it is, man in judgment on the Word of God, one can easily see a fertile theological garden spot in which the seeds of a metaphysical/cosmological philosophy could be sown with disastrous eternal results for those who feast from that garden.

LIBERATION THEOLOGY

Another theology that has exploded like a firecracker on the world scene in the twentieth century is Liberation theology. One of the reasons for its explosive nature is that it tries to couple theology, politics, and social action into one movement to liberate the poor and oppressed people of the world from domination.

This domination is viewed by Liberation exponents as coming from such forces as colonialism; racism; right-wing Christianity; male sexualism, a form of patriarchy where the social order is dominated by the father, the male as the prime definer of authority and power; or any other force, institution, or social movement that could cause oppression upon mankind in general or upon male or female in particular. Yet, the movement or Liberation theology does not flow in one direction only. It branches out into torrents of social protest as streams of action or "praxis" to confront oppression where oppression is seen as the enemy of God.

Praxis or action is paramount in Liberation theology. Robert McAfee Brown, a liberal advocate of Liberation theology, in commenting on Jeremiah 22:13–17 wherein knowing God is to do justice, stated:

> Where, then, will God be found and known? In the doing of justice, in making one's own the cause of the poor, in breaking with systems of oppression, in joining the struggle with the victims.[5]

Liberation theology places great hermeneutical emphasis upon the liberating actions of Jesus in the New Testament and upon the Exodus experience of the Hebrew slaves from their oppression in Egypt as outlined in the Old Testament. The emphasis is on God's action, which is their key to the interpretation of Scripture. As such, Jesus becomes the model to be emulated or imitated in the battle against sin, which is defined by liberationists as social sin that oppresses the poor and all victims of injustice.

These many streams or torrents embodied in this praxis or action of rebellion against any and all types of oppression can be: African Liberation, as seen in South Africa in the life and work of Nelson Mandella; Latin American Liberation, as seen in Gustavo Gutierrez of Peru, and from which many of the other streams obtained their steam; Black Liberation, as seen in the civil rights issues raised by Martin Luther King and others in the last half of the twentieth century in America; Feminist Liberation; Gay Liberation; Palestinian Liberation; or any other movement against what is perceived as oppression.

Is there Marxism in Liberation theology? This has been one of the contentions of its critics. The answer seems to lie mid-way between the extremes. Marxism defines the culture of man as existing between the tension of oppressors and oppressed, so that the conflict is sociological. Liberation theology tries to make the issue theological, yet the entire struggle for liberation can be seen through the eyes of Marxist struggle, the oppressed against the oppressors.

Much of Liberation theology, as seen in the nations comprising South America and Africa, has been well documented. For a change of pace, but not of intent, a definition of Liberation theology as a "Theology of Struggle" by a Filipino clergyman, Eleazer S. Fernandez, committed to Liberation theology, shows the social-political involvement of the community that is oppressed.

> As basically a reflective act within a faith commitment, the theology of struggle has as its objective the enhancing and sharpening of the struggle. It is not so much about God-talk or God-language as it is about "God-walk" or God-praxis or theopraxis in the struggle. The theology of struggle seeks to convey an understanding of theology in which the context—that of the suffering and the struggle of the people—is the primary *locus theologicus,* which is interpreted through the agency of various critical theories and discerned through the eyes of faith. The theology of struggle is a contextual theology, taking "Filipinoness" (inculturation) in light of its larger background—Asian—within the purview of social transformation (liberation thrust).
>
> Moreover, the theology of struggle sees theological reflection more as a community activity, with some individuals having a native charisma of articulation and writing, whereas others have acquired skills through the years of studies. But they all derive their inspiration from the spirit of the community.[6]

While the objective of Liberation theology is commendable in helping the poor and the oppressed of this world, just as Biblical Christianity itself does; nevertheless, there is a wide gulf fixed between the two.

Some points of difference are:

1 Jesus is seen by LT (Liberation Theology) as the model, the human revealer of God, and not as BCT (Biblical Christian Theology) believes in Him as Redeemer, the eternal Son of God for the redemption

of all mankind, the oppressed as well as the oppressors.

2 LT diminishes the theology of the Cross. LT views sin as social sin against the oppressed, while BCT sees sin not only toward the neighbor, but primarily against God. In LT, man defines what sin is. In BCT, God is the definer of sin as He has revealed its meaning in the death of His Son upon the Cross and in His Word in Scripture.

3 In LT, theology must be contextual, that is, intrinsically connected to a specific social situation of oppression. In BCT, theology is universal in that our God as Creator, Redeemer, and Sanctifier is one God over all.

4 In LT, the justification of man before God requires praxis—requires becoming the liberator, doing the action for the benefit of the oppressed. In BCT, justification before God is by faith in Jesus. Article IV of the Augsburg Confession simply, but completely, gives this definition of justification by faith:

> Also they teach that men cannot be justified before God by their own strength, merits, or works, but are freely justified for Christ's sake, through faith, when they believe that they are received into favor and that their sins are forgiven for Christ's sake, who by His death has made satisfaction for our sins. This faith God imputes for righteousness in His sight. Romans 3 and 4.[7]

In order to understand what true liberation is, the above concept from God's Word is the hermeneutical factor that must be considered.

5 In LT, the Scriptures are used in part for liberation purposes, so as to liberate the Word of God, so it

can be used to liberate the oppressed of the world, oppressed by a powerful elite, corrupt power organizations, or by nations who live by class or race distinctions. In BCT, Holy Scripture is the inerrant and infallible Word of God, the norm for all orthodox Christian doctrine. Scripture must be regarded as a whole, and not referred to in pieces or portions apart from the whole.

Carlos Mestes shows the use of the Scriptures in Liberation theology in this way:

> The people's main interest is not to interpret the Bible, but to interpret life with the help of the Bible. They try to be faithful, not primarily to the meaning the text has in itself (the historical and literal meaning), but to the meaning they discover in the text for their lives.[8]

This use of the Scriptures in a conditional way reveals that Liberation theology is bound up in the immanence of this world apart from the transcendence of God. Immanence and transcendence were discussed in Chapter 6 where it was shown that Holy Scripture reveals a balance that the historical-critical method can tip toward the immanence of God over His transcendence.

Does Liberation theology stand in judgment over the Word of God? Does the Word of God stand in clarity as God's propositional revelation? Or have theologians, who are committed to Liberation theology, used the Word of God so that confusion and deception is brought to that Word? The historical-critical method of biblical interpretation lives on.

Feminist Theology

Another user of the historical critical method is Feminist theology, which has focused its main attention upon what is defined as male oppression upon women. While feminists such as Elisabeth Schüssler Fiorenza argue that any traditional interpretation of the Bible, as well as the historical-critical method, must be abandoned;[9] nevertheless, they opt to stand as judge and jury upon all of Scripture. This is exactly what the historical-critical method has attempted to do.

Feminist theology arrived on the theological scene in the late 1960s along with Liberation theology. It views the entire history of Christianity, including the history of the Jews spelled out in the Old Testament, as patriarchal oppression of women. This oppression is described as *patriarchal*—the supremacy of the father in society and religion, and also as *androcentric*—meaning that men are regarded as the center of dignity, virtue, and power, while women are seen as inferior, second-rate, or less worthy than men. Another word used by feminists to describe their oppression is *misogyny*, which is the hatred of women by men.

This oppression by men is viewed as evil, an evil not only in secular society, but also in the Christian and Hebrew religions. Feminists maintain this oppression can only be overcome by the full liberation of women from the dominance of men, not only in the social sector, but also in the religious realm.

One of the main targets of Feminist theology is Holy Scripture, which is viewed as patriarchal, androcentric, and misogynist. Because Holy Scripture is viewed as the basis for Christian theology, Feminist theology looks for another base from which to build its theology; that base is comprised of women's experience, as that experience is defined by feminists. The definition of that experience has as its goal the liberation of women from male dominance. Therefore, the Bible must undergo reconstruction—be edited and reinterpreted—so that the feminist definition of what constitutes biblical truth can overcome the patriarchal, androcentric, and misogynist views of the Bible.

Not only must the Bible be changed, but also the church, which interprets and teaches biblical concepts must be changed. The Christian church that is committed to God's Word in Scripture as truth, is repugnant or antagonistic to feminists. Rosemary Radford Ruether claims, "The more one becomes a feminist the more difficult it becomes to go to church".[10]

The range of corrections proposed by Feminist theology on the Bible is so extensive that only a flavor can be considered here. Elisabeth Schüssler Fiorenza, in discussing Christian feminist apologetics, the defense of the Christian feminist's view of the Bible, stated:

> A Christian feminist apologetics asserts that the Bible, correctly understood, does not prohibit, but rather authorizes the equal rights and liberation of women. This approach usually focuses on "key" passages about women such as Genesis 1–3, the biblical laws with regard to women, or Pauline and Post-Pauline statements about women's place and role, in order to show that they have been misunderstood or misused by those arguing against women's dignity and rights. A feminist hermeneutics, therefore, has the task of elaborating the correct understanding of such texts so that their biblical authority can be claimed for women's rights.[11]

Fiorenza also gave this view:

> Recognizing the pervasive androcentric character of biblical texts, other feminists seek explicitly to isolate an

> authoritative essence or central principle that biblically authorizes equal rights and liberation struggles. Such a liberation hermeneutics does not aim to dislodge the authority of the Bible. On the contrary, it seeks to reclaim the empowering authority of Scripture in order to use it over and against conservative right-wing biblical anti-feminism.[12]

A correction to the traditional Christian church by the feminists is the establishment of the "women-church" as the community of both women and men who are identified with women's struggles. In the women-church setting, they can share the abuses of their oppression and can formulate their opposition to biblical male oppression through the creation of female spirituality, liturgy, and statements about liberation from male domination, biblically and culturally.

This emphasis upon the women-church is a movement away from the traditional Christian church, both Roman Catholic and Protestant. It is within this setting that Fiorenza proposes one of her hermeneutical strategies—establishing a canon within the canon. This concept of a canon within the canon will be discussed later in Chapter 15, but for now, a look at what Fiorenza calls the fourth hermeneutical strategy is most revealing concerning how feminist theology would rearrange, edit, or reconstruct the revelation of God in Holy Scripture.

> A fourth hermeneutical strategy purposes that women-church must create a feminist *Third Testament* that canonizes women's experiences of G-d's presence as a new textual base. Revelatory breakthrough experiences inspire women to write new poems and tell new stories which are given authority by the base communities of women-church. Feminist theology authenticates these stories and thereby "creates a new textual base, a new

> canon," a "Third Testament" that can speak about the experience of G-d's presence in the lives of women. "Women must be able to speak out of their own experiences of agony and victimization, survival, empowerment and new life, as places of divine presence, and out of these revelatory experiences write new stories." Just as the androcentric texts of the First and Second Testaments reflect male experience, so also the stories rooted in women's experience constitute a Third Testament which deserves canonical status.[13]

Not only do Feminist theologians reconstruct and add to Holy Scripture, they also abandon the doctrine of the Holy Trinity. Bradley C. Hanson is Professor of Religion at Luther College in Decorah, Iowa, a college affiliated with the ELCA. In a textbook for college students on Christian theology, he relates that the male imagery of the Trinity, as seen by feminists, has supported male domination.

Hanson tells of three differing views of the Trinity by feminists. First, he refers to Mary Daly who maintains that Christianity has been so deeply corrupted by patriarchy that women should completely abandon Christianity—the Trinity included—and create a new religion that affirms the woman, using theologies from other religions that affirm a Goddess over a male God. Second, he refers to Sally McFague who sees a transcendent God as a controlling Father figure who must be seen in the light of immanence rather than transcendence, all the while rejecting Jesus as God's Son and holding Him to be only a great teacher.

In place of the Trinity, McFague would substitute three metaphors that reinterpret the Trinity and which emphasize God's immanence: Mother, Lover, Friend.

Hanson gave as the third view, the interpretation of Catherine Mowry LaCugna, an interpretation with which he agreed. In place of the Trinitarian language of Father, Son, and Holy Spirit, LaCugna proposed: Mother-Daughter, Father-Daughter, Mother-Son, Lover-Beloved, and Friend-Friend. Hanson also stated:

> . . . to use only male metaphors for God does give the impression that God is male and does tend to support male domination in church and society. Thus it is generally beneficial for Christians to refer to God with a variety of terms, as long as the whole context of use has a clear linkage with the biblical story. In addition to calling God Father, it is appropriate to speak of God as Mother and like a woman in some respects.[14]

Feminists have renamed God so that He is often referred to as God/ess, She, Her, Mother-Goddess, Sophia, G-d Sophia, G-d-Sophia-Sapienta-Wisdom, and the other similar terms. In taking the maleness out of God, they also must take Jesus as a male out of the Trinity and make Him simply a teacher—certainly not Son of God.

Gail Ramshaw, Associate Professor of Religion at LaSalle University in Philadelphia, and a member of the ELCA, in the interest of reforming God-language in the liturgy of Christian worship, revealed the feminist conception of Jesus. This constitutes a reconstruction of orthodox biblical revelation wherein Jesus as Son of God is never disputed. Ramshaw, however, takes exception and stated:

> The Christian belief that God became incarnate in a male human being has fueled an androcentric bias that occasionally tries to defend masculinity inherent in God. . . . To equate God with the man Jesus is to delete women from the story of salvation.
>
> From the vantage point of the twentieth century, the orthodox strategy to keep the second person equal with

> the first appears to have failed. The intention, to raise the incarnate Christ to God, ironically resulted in the opposite: God was demoted to the level of a man.[15]

Ramshaw further commented on the preference of God-the-mother language over God-the- father language:

> What is so intriguing about God-the-mother language is that it has become far more physically explicit than God-the-father language ever was. Catechesis, mystagogy, homiletics, and hymnody now praise God's womb and breasts, although the Christian tradition never praised God's penis or testicles.[16]

For those denominations who believe that Scripture is the Word of God, the feminist thrust in theology is not a threat because Feminist theology has so manipulated and negated the Scriptures, and the Scriptures' revelation of who Jesus is, that their theological position is viewed as foreign and unacceptable, if not heretical. Feminist theology presents a problem for denominations which still hold to some degree that Scripture contains the Word of God. Denominations that embrace the historical-critical method fall into that category. One such denomination that finds itself caught up in trying to balance a scriptural theological position based on the historical-critical method and the theology of feminism is the ELCA.

Beverly J. Stratton of Augsburg College in Minneapolis, Minnesota, in an article entitled, *Here We Stand: Lutheran and Feminist Issues in Biblical Interpretation*, stated the dilemma of biblical interpretation that is posed in the mixture of the ELCA's interpretation and that of feminist theology. Stratton looked at the nature of the Bible and in so doing gave an accurate accounting of how her church, the ELCA, views Scripture. She acknowledged that the feminist view may differ from ELCA's view. She wrote:

> The nature of the Bible is one area where Lutheran and feminist interpreters may differ. The premodern understanding of Scripture as divine revelation, authored by the Holy Spirit, and the very Word of God, gave way in the modern period to a view that acknowledges the results of historical criticism: Scripture was written by fallible humans who witness to God's revelation. In this view, the Bible is not revelation and Word of God itself; instead it is an occasion for revelation and a vehicle for the Word of God to be heard once again. Rather than being a "transubstantiated" text, modern scholars affirm the Scriptures as another instance of the finite being capable of the infinite. We have the "treasure" of the Word of God in the "earthen vessels" of the human documents of Scripture, used by God as they are. The texts themselves are the swaddling cloths and manger for God's law and gospel. The qualitative difference between Scripture and other literature is not its divine authorship but the role it has held in the Christian Church by mediating God's Word.[17]

Stratton pointed out that the feminist view of Scripture, which opposes God being presented and portrayed in masculine terms, makes the Bible, which has been recognized as "good news for modern man," bad news for modern women. Stratton, in trying to bring together the historical-critical method and the feminist view of Scripture, offered a correlation. Can this be a use of correlation that Paul Tillich proposed as in synthesis?

> Feminists and Lutherans participate in the world and are concerned that our listeners hear the gospel when we proclaim it. Hence we affirm some principle of correlation; we read with the Bible in one hand and the newspaper or World Wide Web in the other. Additional feminist agreements with Lutherans depend on whether Lutherans allow modern historical consciousness to affect their understanding of Scripture.[18]

Stratton's conclusion was most interesting and optimistic in scope.

> The Lutheran Confessions were able to presume the authority of Scripture without explicitly stating it as dogma. For Scripture to continue to function authoritatively in the twenty-first century for a church informed by feminist scholarship, Lutheran Christians will need to clarify our understandings of the nature of Scripture and the role of interpretation. We should consider whether *Sola Scriptura* can be maintained in view of the Enlightenment's insistence on reason. We may acknowledge that the Holy Spirit guided authors, editors, text critics, translators, and interpreters of Scripture for the church, but we must also observe and consider the implications of their fallible human and often androcentric or misogynist work. We may reiterate the reformers' insistence that Scripture interprets itself, but we must be able to explain what this means in a context where people from different social locations hear and understand the text differently from one another. We should clarify how Scripture is our authoritative source and norm, articulating general principles consistent with (or reasonably against) modern or postmodern consciousness, and explaining the relationship among interpretation, advocacy, and praxis. Finally,

> we need to develop an ethics of interpretation, so that our preaching from and teaching about the Scripture do not obstruct its proclamation of law and gospel. We engage in this work boldly, confident in the power of the Holy Spirit that God's Word forever shall prevail.[19]

When a scholar familiar with the Scriptures looks at Feminist theology, the conclusion can be none other than an appraisal which shows that its concern is with a reconstruction of Scripture. In this reconstruction, male sexism is eliminated and the oppression of women by Scripture is eradicated so that a dominant feminist role may emerge in the theological and social world of post-modern reality. The authority of Scripture, in any traditional sense, has been negated and thrown out, as the control of Scripture has been passed to Feminist theologians whose aim is clearly to rewrite Scripture according to the feminine image.

As stated above, this presents a "dicey" problem for mainline denominations committed to the historical-critical method who have opened their theological and scriptural doors to Feminist theology. How do they reconcile Feminist theology with their mission of preaching Jesus Christ as Savior? Are they ready to make more radical changes to the interpretation of Scripture?

Feminist theology does not proclaim the Christian faith, but a totally different religion. How sad it is that feminists have great difficulty in praising and confessing Jesus as Philippians 2:10–11 declares: "that at the name of Jesus EVERY KNEE SHOULD BOW, of those who are in heaven, and on the earth, and under the earth, and that every tongue should confess that Jesus is Lord, to the glory of God the Father."

Deception? Confusion? I have emphasized these words, beginning with the Enlightenment and continuing to our present age, to show how God's inerrant and infallible Word has been attacked, twisted, denied, and used according to presuppositions that do not honor or bless our God: Father, Son, and Holy Spirit, or the propositional revelation of His truth in Holy Scripture. Will this confusion and deception ever end? As long as sinful man can challenge God as being God, it will continue. Other attacks on God's Word will invade and impact upon the theological arena of biblical hermeneutics as scholars continue to alter and sit in judgment upon the Word of God as revealed in Holy Scripture.

The Jesus Seminar

I have saved the Jesus Seminar for the last example of a modern attempt to question the Word of God. In 1993, Macmillan, New York, published *The Five Gospels: The Search for the Authentic Words of Jesus* by Robert W. Funk, Roy W. Hoover, and the Jesus Seminar. It was the culmination of six years of critical study concerning the authenticity of the words of Jesus in the Gospels of Matthew, Mark, Luke, and John. The seminar's study did not stop there. It included what they called the "Gospel of Thomas," writings which were not and are not included in the Bible, writings preserved in a Coptic version as part of the Nag Hammadi Codices that were discovered in Upper Egypt in 1945. Thus, a "fifth" gospel was added to the pot.

The seminar was co-chaired by Funk of Westar Institute and John Dominic Crossan of De Paul University in Chicago and was comprised of over seventy researchers and theologians. They met at various locations, such as the Pacific School of Religion in Berkeley, California and the Roman Catholic Saint Meinrad Archabbey in St. Meinrad, Indiana. Were there Lutheran professors and theologians associated with this venture? Sadly, yes. Listed as "Fellows of the Jesus Seminar" were: ELCA professors, Dr. Arland Jacobson of Concordia College, Moorhead,

Minnesota; Dr. Richard L. Jeske and Dr. Robert D. Kysar of the Lutheran Theological Seminary at Philadelphia.[20] Not all the members of the seminar were in attendance at every meeting, as the average was about thirty participants per session.

The seminar concentrated on the democratic procedure of voting, conducted after discussion and debate, so that an evaluation of authenticity could be given to the approximately 1,500 statements of Jesus in the four Gospels of the New Testament and in the added gospel of Thomas. Their method of voting was by the use of colored beads dropped into a box for each and every statement or saying of Jesus. *The San Diego Union* reported:

> Seminar scholars came together several times to debate and vote, dropping color-coded beads into a box: red was a vote for authenticity, pink meant it sounded like something Jesus would say, gray was an ambivalent maybe and black was something Jesus definitely did not say. "We tended to do the black stuff by consensus . . . but we really did debate the ones that we finally colored red and pink" says Funk, a longtime religious studies teacher and author who retired from the University of Montana in 1986.
>
> That color coding carried over into the pages of "The Five Gospels," where "the authentic words" are written in red ink, becoming an eerie parody of the popular editions of the Bible where Jesus' words are printed in red. Most of the pages, however, are solid black with smatterings of pink and gray paragraphs, sentences, or in some cases, single words.[21]

Following are some examples of the voting, and criteria for voting, on certain Bible verses:

"For God so loved the world that he gave his only Son, so that everyone who believes in him may not perish but may have eternal life". (John 3:16) Black. This entire speech, they argue, probably embodies that evangelist's version of Christianity.

"Go therefore and make disciples of all nations, baptizing them in the name of the Father and of the Son and of the Holy Spirit . . . And remember, I am with you always, to the end of the age." (Matthew 28:19–20) Black. This great commission smacks too much of the work of individual evangelists wanting to push the Jesus movement more than the humble carpenter interested in individual behavior, according to the scholars. Jesus, they say, probably had no idea of launching a world mission and was not an institution-builder.

"You shall love your neighbor as yourself."(Matthew 22:39) Gray. The seminar fellows are at odds over this one. Some say it sounds too much like what one of Jesus' rivals, a rabbi named Hillel, said. Others say it certainly fits with some of his other thoughts. So they compromised on gray.[22]

The startling and shocking result of the Jesus Seminar is a denial of about eighty percent of the words that Holy Scripture attributes to Jesus. That this "scholarly" procedure and its results came from the groundwork laid by the historical-critical method can not be denied.

Theologians standing in judgment upon Jesus' words in the Four Gospels of the New Testament, along with an "added" gospel, are living proof that they are "scholarly" descendants of Johann Salomo Semler of the eighteenth century. Semler saw as his scholarly obligation, the challenge of finding what could be the Word of God in Scripture, just as the Jesus Seminar attempted to find authentic words of Jesus in the Gospels. Confusion and deception in regard to Holy Scripture being the Word of God has not faded from the theological arena of battle.

Notes

1. John B. Cobb, Jr. and David Ray Griffin, *Process Theology: An Introductory Exposition,* (Philadelphia: The Westminster Press, 1976), 102–103.
2. David Basinger, *Divine Power in Process Theology,* (Albany: State University of New York Press, 1988), 7.
3. John B. Cobb, Jr., *God and the World,* (Philadelphia: The Westminster Press, 1965), 116.
4. David Basinger, op. cit., 7–8.
5. Robert McAfee Brown, *Unexpected News; Reading the Bible with Third World Eyes,* (Philadelphia: The Westminster Press, 1984), 69.
6. Eleazer S. Fernandez, *Toward a Theology of Struggle,* (New York: Orbis Books, 1994), 168.
7. *Book of Concord,* (St. Louis: Concordia Publishing House, 1950), 12–13.
8. Carlos Mestes, *Defenseless Flower: A New Reading of the Bible,* trans. Francis McDonagh, (Marynoll, New York: Orbis Books, 1989), 9.
9. Elisabeth Schüssler Fiorenza, *But SHE Said: Feminist Practices of Biblical Interpretation,* (Boston: Beacon Press, 1992), 139.
10. Rosemary Radford Ruether, *Sexism and God-Talk: Toward a Feminist Theology,* (Boston: Beacon Press, 1983), 193–194.
11. Elisabeth Schüssler Fiorenza, op. sit.,144–145.
12. Ibid., 146–147.
13. Ibid., 148–149.
14. Bradley C. Hanson, *Introduction to Christian Theology,* (Minneapolis: Fortress Press, 1997), 38–41.
15. Gail Ramshaw, *God Beyond Gender,* (Minneapolis: Fortress Press, 1995), 31.

16. Ibid., 37.

17. Beverly J. Stratton, *Here We Stand: Lutheran and Feminist Issues in Biblical Interpretation,*vol. 24, no.1, (*Currents in Theology and Mission*, February 1997), 24.

18. Ibid., 29–30.

19. Ibid., 32.

20. Herman Otten, (*Christian News*, 2 January 1989), 1.

21. "Sandi Dolbee, Tarnished Words", *San Diego Union,* 4 February 1994, Currents Section E, p. 4.

22. Ibid, 4.

Chapter 12

King of the Mountain

But know this first of all, that no prophecy of Scripture is a matter of one's own interpretation, for no prophecy was ever made by an act of human will, but men moved by the Holy Spirit spoke from God. (2 Pet. 1:20, 21)

In the preceding chapters, you have encountered theologians and philosophers who, in questioning the Word of God, have acted like drunken sailors. They reel and stagger, intoxicated with their own views, while disregarding not only the possibility, but the fact and reality that God has spoken His truth in and through His Word by the power of the Holy Spirit. That there is a disconnectedness can not be disputed. Just read or listen to their words, words that do not honor or bless Holy Scripture as true Word of God.

One who is more than qualified to make a reality appraisal of what has transpired on the recent stage of biblical hermeneutics is Dr. John Macquarrie. He is formerly a professor at Union Theological Seminary, New York and

Professor Emeritus of Divinity in the University of Oxford, England. He provided a survey of twentieth century religious thought in which the diversity of thinking in theology and philosophy has had a confusing effect on religious thought. He began to bring to conclusion his survey with these words:

> At the end of the survey, the reader may well feel somewhat bewildered. We have met so many views of religion, some of them sharply conflicting, others shading off into each other, and some of them so diverse that they seem to be talking about quite different things or at any rate very different aspects of the same thing. Out of this teeming diversity, no common view emerges. At the beginning of the book we quoted the remarks made by an English theologian (J. R. Illingworth, my inclusion) at the beginning of the century, in which he pointed to a "multitude of incoherent and incompatible points of view, all of which may be called modern, but none of which can claim to be typically representative of the age—currents and cross-currents and rapids and backwaters of thought."[1]

"No common view emerges . . ." and while those words are spoken about theology and religious thought, they are hermeneutical words which bounce off the Holy Scriptures of God, His Word, from which true Christian theology emerges, doctrine that coincides with Scripture and is not in opposition to it. "Bewildered, diverse, incoherent, incompatible" are the descriptive words used by Macquarrie regarding the "currents and cross-currents and rapids and backwaters of thought," a living indictment of the historical-critical method of biblical interpretation.

Negative words are the only words available when critics committed to historical criticism confront the Word of God, head on. They have little blessing and honor to render to Almighty God: Father, Son, and Holy Spirit. Why? Because they are caught up in a power struggle for authority, a power struggle to have "one-upmanship" on God and His Word, a struggle from the Garden of Eden to the day in which we live. "And the beat goes on . . ."

The quest for authority, which is the quest for power, never ceases. It never disappears. The everyday business, political, social, educational, and professional world is the setting for this struggle for authority and power. There is never a time, so it seems, when some force, movement, or person is not vying for control, for power. You and I have been spectators of many power struggles in the world, but when it comes to a contest for power in regard to spiritual matters and the Bible, most of us have not been informed. If we have seen some comment in the newspapers, usually it has been the Sunday religion section that has made note of it, but it seldom makes front-page headlines.

In my youth, a favorite game played by adolescent boys was "King of the Mountain." In this game, usually the strongest lad would position himself at the top of a hill and would try to repel all challenges from lads of lesser strength and stature. If and when replaced as the king of the mountain, another lad would assume the power place until he was toppled, and the game would go on and on until our strength ebbed, or we thought it time to do something else athletically in our quest for macho recognition.

Whether we have been aware of it or not, the game described above is played for scholarly theological recognition. It takes place in the out-of-view world of hermeneutics, behind seminary classroom doors, in religious periodicals, and in books of theology in which the sophisticated terminology of philosophers and theologians act as a secret code to which the average Christian has little or no access, and perhaps, little or no interest. That is, until a major theological "bomb" is dropped in their midst, like the draft of a task force study in 1993 by the ELCA, entitled "The Church and Human Sexuality: A Lutheran Perspective."

The draft dropped the "bomb" in its twenty-one page report, which received coverage by the Associated Press (AP). The AP article said in its opening paragraph, quoting the draft, that "masturbation is healthy, the Bible supports homosexual unions, and teaching teens how to use condoms to prevent disease is a moral imperative".[2]

The uproar that followed in ELCA congregations when asked to review the draft was deafening. Could this have been an indication that a majority of the laity, the church members, still viewed Holy Scripture as the Word of God? Such a study with conclusions *that were more than suggestions* is totally off the wall and completely incompatible with the truth of sexuality to which Holy Scripture witnesses, and as such, was another anomaly contrary to the truth of God in His Holy Word. It stands as another product of the historical-critical method of confusion and deception of the Word of God.

Not only was there an uproar in ELCA congregations, but also in LCMS congregations. When AP made its report, it went along with the inclusive words of the draft that indicated that this was the position of all Lutherans when it stated,"A Lutheran Perspective," the last words of the title of the draft. The ELCA move was a "king-of-the-mountain" move, as it tried to convey its non-scriptural findings and assertions to the religious world as well as to the secular world, which would devour it as authentic truth and applaud its modern, trendy, and "realistic" view as that of all Lutherans.

In response both to ELCA's position and the report of AP to the world regarding the draft, the LCMS made quick reply on 20 October 1993 in a press release sent to national media and local media organizations. *Reporter,* an official publication of the LCMS gave the context of that response in this way:

> In reporting the contents of the draft statement, some newspapers ran headlines that referred to the ELCA by using the more generic term "Lutheran." . . . *The Dallas Morning News,* for example, ran a headline saying, "Lutheran group unveils sexuality report." . . . *The Chicago Tribune,* on the other hand, said "Lutheran sex report puts emphasis on love." . . . In St. Louis, the *Post-Dispatch* said, "Lutheran Panel Supports Masturbation, Gay Couples."
>
> While the headlines are generally accurate, LCMS officials said they felt people could get the impression that all Lutherans supported homosexuality and masturbation.
>
> The Synod, therefore, issued a press statement saying, in part: "The Lutheran Church-Missouri Synod, believing that the Bible is God's Word and that the Bible speaks clearly and directly on the matter of proper human sexual behavior, does not—in any way—support homosexual behavior or the idea that masturbation is healthy."
>
> In a separate letter to the St. Louis Post-Dispatch, Dr. Samuel H. Nafzger, executive secretary of the Synod's Commission on Theology and Church Relations, took exception to the newspaper's headline, saying in part: . . . "While this headline may correctly describe the position of a panel of the Evangelical Lutheran Church in America, it most certainly does not present the position of The Lutheran Church-Missouri Synod or any of its entities on the issue. . . . It is important that we as Missouri-Synod Lutherans, say clearly that we neither concur with nor

> support the conclusions of the ELCA task force report," said Synod President A. L. Barry.[3]

Another king-of-the-mountain tactic widely used in denominations committed to the historical-critical method is to use the academic position of the scholar as the epitome, the embodiment, of final authority regarding God's Word. What happens is this: The function of authority over the Word of God is transferred from Almighty God, to the scholar. Authority does not evaporate or simply disappear. It has simply been transferred to, or usurped by, the scholar.

In this process, one usually finds the scholar not looking to God, but to the world and its wisdom, its philosophy, for clues of interpretation and emphasis, which will have appeal and meaning to a secular culture. I met this first hand in my seminary experience as some of my fellow students thought it to be of utmost importance to have a handle on Kierkegaard, Barth, Brunner, or Tillich, rather than God's Word. To be able to rattle off quotes from scholars, and have professors sanction the authority of such theological or philosophical positions, were the "Atta boy!" encouragements that some young seminarians feasted upon.

When one reads post-modern theology today, the king-of-the-mountain theory of power and authority has not only been transferred to biblical scholars who are supposed to have the last word—the epitome of revelation concerning God and truth—but sadly, the theory of power and authority has been transferred to the secular world and its categories of importance and the truth which it defines. Scholars have used secular wisdom and philosophy only to find that what they used became the platforms for a theology, ruled and normed by the secular.

Instead of God and His Word being the source of Christian theology, secular sources and forces are made to stand as authorities and are given places of importance as new authoritative sources of post-modern spiritual enlightenment. There is quite a fraternity and sorority of post-modern biblical scholars who dance together in mutual support and admiration. What they dance away from, however, is Holy Scripture as the Word of God. David F. Wells has commented on this situation by giving an example of Robert Schuller. He wrote:

> In another age, Robert Schuller's ministry, for example, might well have been viewed not as Christian ministry at all, but as comedy. Would it not be possible to view him as providing a biting parody of American self-absorption? Sin, he says with a cherubic smile, "is not what shatters our relationship to God; the true culprit is the jaundiced eye we have turned on ourselves. The problem is that we do not esteem ourselves enough. In the Crystal Cathedral, therefore, let the word *sin* be banished, whether in song, Scripture, or prayer. There is never any confession there. Then again, Christ was not drawing a profound moral compass in the Sermon on the Mount; he was just giving us a set of 'be (happy) attitudes.'" The word was, don't worry, be happy. And God is not so mean as to judge; he is actually very amiable and benign. Comedy this devastating would be too risky for most to attempt. But Schuller is no comic. He earnestly wants us to believe all of this, and many do. When he makes these pronouncements, he attracts a large and devoted Christian following. What is the appeal?[4]

Wells answered his question by saying that the appeal is to ride the stream of modernity.

To ride the tide, what an indictment! That, however, is the power-push of post-modern theology wherein scholars in love with new trends, latch on to them and spawn them into theories that have no semblance to what God proclaims in His Holy Word.

An interesting assessment of the modern theologian is by Ted Peters in his book, *GOD—The World's Future.* When this book was written, Peters was Professor of Systematic Theology at Pacific Lutheran Theological Seminary and the Graduate Theological Union, Berkeley, California. He prefaced his assessment by describing a beautiful church of rococo style in Bavaria, in southern Germany, the Wieskirche, which was built to proclaim the Gospel of Jesus against any and all attacks of the Enlightenment. The artist, Johann Baptist Zimmerman, painted biblical scenes in grandeur upon the walls and ceiling of the church.

Having visited this beautiful church with my wife some years ago, one scene etched upon both our hearts and minds is the eyes of the Lord as they are seen from the front of the nave when looking back toward the narthex. No matter where we walked, the eyes of the Lord followed us. Could this have been the artist's call to the clergy, facing the people of God, to be faithful to God's Word?

Peters stated that the Bavarian kings of the eighteenth and nineteenth centuries wanted this part of Germany to become

> . . . an island of naive if not reactionary faith that sought to protect itself from the strong currents of the modern world swirling about it.
>
> In the twentieth century the island of safety has been sorely eroded. The tides of modern life are everywhere sweeping away traditional verities. So, like the Bavarian kings before them, many people of Christian faith throughout the world today wonder if there can be—or even if there ought to be—a safe island of belief that will

> not be washed away by the eroding eddies of the modern mind.[5]

This was his setting for his assessment of the modern theologian.

> One can identify the modern theologian as a person who is willing to jump off the island and attempt to swim amid the currents of modern consciousness. He or she is aware of the risks of leaving the dry land of biblical naivete behind, but hopes that farther out to sea another island of meaning will appear. If none does appear, then perhaps with strong faith one can simply learn to enjoy the unending swim.[6]

That may well be an assessment or definition of a modern theologian committed to the historical-critical method, but certainly not one committed to Scripture as the Word of God, inerrant and infallible. There is no hesitation, doubt, or wavering whatsoever in the theologian who knows in faith that the Holy Scriptures are God's Word. He can address the people of God in direct, propositional language from God, regarding their lives and the living of their lives. He doesn't need to take a Kierkegaardian leap or a plunge with the probability of an "unending swim."

If theologians who make that leap are not confused and deceived, then the people of God watching them, people like you who look for the certainty and truthfulness of their God, can see the confusion. Just maybe, the people of God don't want to leave "the dry land of biblical naivete" behind. Modern theologians, the swim is all yours!

And why are modern or post-modern theologians swimming? Could it be that they are looking to the currents and riptides of post-modern world thought, while trying to fashion a theology that will fit post-modern times, and so rescue the people of God, whom they view as "adrift" and "flailing" in such currents and riptides?

The currents and riptides of a secular society, such as the one in which we live, can be said to include *pluralism, doubt,* and *secularism* itself. Other categories can be defined, but for the person who comes to worship Almighty God, as well as the person who has yet to be brought by the Holy Spirit to the joy of worshipping Him, these categories have substance. They are the categories into which much of post-modern theological thought has been stuffed. They represent the world in which we live. As such, post-modern theologians give them places of power when making theological definitions. Their relevance to post-modern theology far supersedes God's Word in Holy Scripture. The king-of-the-mountain theory of power is there in the invasion of the secular into and over the sacred.

In the theological arena, pluralism is a word often used to describe the multifaceted world of religions: Christianity, Judaism, Buddhism, Hinduism, Islam, and whatever other "isms" emerge as religions. Pluralism is a popular word in a world that reveres diversity as the path to truth. Because there has been a shift by way of the Enlightenment in the way people look at truth from an objective to a subjective view, we have a whole new ball game in the theological arena.

Pluralism, by its very nature, renders a neutral evaluation of all religions. All stand on level ground, not one in dominance above the others. If all can be considered to have some semblance of truth, maybe articulated in different ways but with evidence of sincerity, then their validity can be established as viable religions for mankind. Therefore, pluralism has no place for the objective truth of God in Holy Scripture, which is Christ-centered.

This stance can be seen today in a pluralistic society in America that condemns Christians who hold in faith that Scripture is the inerrant and infallible Word of God and who live by that Word. Such Christians are labeled as "biblicists," "fundamentalists," and yes, the "religious right," all of which are the words that fit into a negative, post-modern, politically-correct definition of what it means to be a Christian.

David F. Wells has exposed the heresy of pluralism in Christianity in these words:

> . . . the New Testament does not allow for the possibility of pursuing the new pluralistic theological strategy of moving away from Christ-centered faith toward God-centered faith. The reason, quite simply, is that the incarnation is fundamentally important: we know God only through Jesus. The permanent bonding of divine and human in Christ cannot be sundered. It is unacceptable to claim that Christ is anonymously manifested in other religions that specifically deny the particularity of that revelation in Christ. . . . The New Testament christology is a christology from above. How else would he have been able to reveal the nature and will of his Father? A Christ who was less than pre-existent, less than fully divine, or unaware of who he was would not have been able to reveal the Father or to redeem sinners.
>
> The only way in which we can be God-centered, then, is to be Christ-centered, for God is salvifically known nowhere else (Acts 2: 36–38; 4: 12; 13: 26–41; 17: 29–31). It is popularly argued to the contrary that to be Christ-centered is to be other than God-centered because it excludes all religious options other than Christianity and hence excludes much of what God is doing in the world

> today. Whatever the attractions of this argument, it is simply unscriptural. It makes the reality of God diffuse, assails the uniqueness of his revelation in Christ, dispenses with Christ's saving death, and upends the premise of the entire biblical narrative, which is that God alone has reality, while the gods and goddesses of the pagans are nonentities. The New Testament unequivocally sounds the note of Christ's uniqueness, the clarion call of historical particularity, which vitiates every other religious claim.[7]

Louis A. Smith, pastor of St. Paul's Lutheran Church, Collingswood, New Jersey, gave an interesting report regarding the second "Continuing Reformation" conference of the ELCA, held in November of 1995 in Philadelphia. One of the workshop presenters was a theologian from the Lutheran Theological Seminary at Philadelphia, Dr. Paul Rajashekar. The workshop was called "Reforming the Church's Ministry Amid Religious Pluralism."

A portion of Smith's report in *Lutheran Forum* centered on this workshop.

> Rajashekar begins from the "fact" of sociological pluralism, which has altered America's landscape. No longer do we meet only other Christians but Muslims, Hindus, Buddhists and who knows what else. For Rajashekar this "new reality" has produced several false responses. The first false response is a turn inward and an emphasis on "self-definition." The other responses are rooted in a "xenophobia," a fear of what is foreign. All the Abrahamic faiths have trouble here, he maintains, because all have the notion of the "jealous God." In light of this "fear," some people look to conversion, some treat other religions as peripheral, some with religious neutrality or relativism. The most popular response, he says, is tolerance, which is only

> passive hostility because it is "we" who are doing the tolerating of another.
>
> In the face of this Rajashekar wants us to recognize that our own religion is culture-bound, that religious imperialism presumes an untenable notion of cultural superiority, that Law and Gospel don't work in relation to other religions because it is based on our assumptions about them, and that so called indigenization or contextualization is only another version of an aggressive mind set. Rajashekar's solution to the problem of pluralism is to "redefine Christian Ministry," Word and Sacrament are ok but not sufficient. There must be a public ministry in which the pastor is for all people, even of other faiths, and so must be trained to know other faiths. If the reader is confused, so is the writer. What is clear, however, is that Rajashekar wants us to see Christianity as one option among others. A somewhat vaguely formed "theology of dialogue" and "dialogical understanding of ministry" are invoked as method. We are to discover how other religions "embody faith" and, of course, tell how we do it. But in all of this there seems a shift. What we bear witness to and receive witness about turns out to be our subjective faith, not Christ.[8]

When post-modern liberal pluralism pulls the plug and turns off the power of God's Word in Scripture, what remains is a word-babble residue of pluralistic ideas and options floating in an ever-moving sea of possibilities. Deception and confusion plague the Christian church when possibilities and not certainties are fed to God's people as spiritual food and when evangelical Christian ministry is compromised in the name of pluralism. Doubt emerges.

The riptide of doubt is a clever weapon in the devil's arsenal. He used it to tempt our Lord as shown in both the fourth chapter of Matthew and in the fourth chapter of Luke. In that well-known scene in the wilderness where Jesus was tempted by the devil, there was the implication by the devil of doubt when he questioned Jesus with the conditional words, "If you are the Son of God . . .?" followed by the devil's conditions. He was implying doubt as to the Messiah's identity and His power. This implication of doubt concerning Jesus, His Father, the Holy Spirit, and God's Word in Holy Scripture, continues. It will continue until Jesus comes again.

What you have read in this work of philosophers and theologians has cast shadows of doubt upon God's Word. Kant rejected any transcendent thought of God wherein God is the revealer of His will and love for mankind. Hegel maintained that reality, including the Holy Scriptures, has no constancy and remains an open-ended option of interpretation because it has no fixed standards of right and wrong, no absolutes. Kierkegaard ruled out any truth in the objective certainty of the Bible, and Barth claimed that the Bible can not be revelation, but a witness to the revelation of God, on and on, to Process theologians and Feminist revisionists of Scripture and the Jesus Seminar, all of whom sowed seeds of doubt regarding Scripture as the Word of God.

Not only have philosophers and theologians taken their shots in the doubt department, but add to their salvos, the impact of modern technology through science and medicine. As a result, dependence upon God is pushed further and further away until the deathbed beckons or the foxhole is about to be overrun by the enemy or obliterated by a mortar round. Behavioral sciences such as psychology and sociology have also aided in the doubt fever, elevating man to a position of power as the healing provider, so that God and His Word are not needed or wanted.

Pluralism and doubt are all part of the warp and woof of the fabric of secularism, a subject we know so well because we have grown up in its midst. Its very being dwells within us in our sinful nature. I view secularism as "me" without Jesus as my Lord and Savior and without Holy Scripture as God's message to me, which proclaims and, by the power of the Holy Spirit, lays the faith foundation for Jesus to be my Redeemer and Lord. Certainly secularism involves the indifference to, or the rejection of, God and His Word in any and all areas of life. The Enlightenment influenced scholars to alter the definition, I believe, to encompass the subjective self as the only reality worthy of deification. God and His Word had no place.

In the secular world, it is simply not a question of the interpretation of the Bible as God's Word, but should it exist at all? And this is the battlefield: Who is going to be King of the Mountain? The bottom line has always been, since the Garden of Eden, either God's Word or the devil's suggestion and enticement of rebellion. And you, the reader, and I, the writer, are on the battlefield. Like it or not, we are in the midst of the battle. Who will win? Will we survive? Are there Purple Hearts for the wounded? Is God in Christ really the Savior? In the Enlightenment mode of the subjective self, "Will 'I' survive?"

In my Navy duty, orders took me to two university campuses where I was a student at one and the senior chaplain at the other. I had already spent a year on the Vietnam battlefield as regimental chaplain of the 11th Marines, the artillery regiment in support of the infantry battalions of the 1st Marine Division. I believe that I held more memorial services for Marines killed in action and ministered to more wounded and sick Marines than most parish pastors would minister to parishioners in that same year span.

Every Sunday I traveled the battlefield to artillery battalions and outposts, so that a normal Sabbath for me was at least five worship services, always with the administration of Holy Communion. During the week, I was in helicopters or my jeep transversing the battlefield, ducking sniper bullets and mortar rounds, to offer Holy Communion and give spiritual counsel to Marines and Navy corpsmen in the heat and frustration of battle. There was no such thing as a day off in combat. As I write this, an awareness just surfaced. I was never fired upon on Sunday mornings or afternoons. The evenings were a different story.

I offer the above as background to the battlefield I found on those campuses. Secularism, like war, has casualties. Its casualties do not bleed or, in death, are not placed in body bags. Its casualties suffer from wounded hearts, minds, and spirits that impact upon other lives, as well as their own. Secularism never crowns winners, only victims.

In 1971, a little more than a year after returning from Vietnam, the Navy selected me for postgraduate study in the field of human behavior. I tried to figure out if the Navy was trying to improve my behavior or make me better equipped to improve the Navy's behavior.

In the late summer of 1972, I arrived on the campus of United States International University, San Diego (USIU), a university well endowed in the field of human behavior, with visiting professors like Dr. Viktor E. Frankl. He shared with our class, not only his experiences in Auschwitz, the Nazi death and concentration camp, but also his theories of logotherapy. I can never forget one of his fondest quotes from Nietzsche: "He who has a *why* to live can bear with almost any *how*." I would later find out how correct that statement was and is, from American prisoners of war held in North Vietnam for years, to whom I ministered at the Naval Postgraduate School in Monterey, California.

My intent was to acquire knowledge in the field of human behavior, write a thesis, and receive a master's degree in that field within a span of nine months, the time allotted by the Navy. With God's help, that intent was fulfilled. Yet, my most amazing discovery was not knowledge, but the heart and life conditions of some of the students who were my classmates. When they found out that I was a Navy chaplain (at that time out of uniform, in their "digs" and in the same situation of acquiring an education, fighting for grades), they formed a bond with me. It didn't take long for many of them to disclose to me the wounds of the secular world upon their hearts and lives. For some, the pursuit of education in the field of human behavior was their cry for help and healing.

I thought I had left my pastoral counseling role behind at Naval Station, San Diego, but here I was doing as much, if not more, counseling to the hurting people of God. Somehow, I had never expected this ministry. I thought I was going to be a full-time student, a joy I seized with great expectation. But God had another ministry for me, one totally unexpected.

He opened my eyes and heart to His people outside the churches I served, and outside of the naval establishment of Navy and Marine Corps personnel. Here were well-dressed students who were financially comfortable with the "things" of this world, but many were bound up by secular wounds to heart, mind, and spirit. They were like the wounded in need of healing, to whom I ministered on Vietnam's battlefields.

The spiritual care I offered was from God's Word and not from the human behavioral sciences of our studies. I had learned, long before this educational experience, that psychology and the behavioral sciences are experts in diagnosing the illness, the wounds, but helpless in trying "to put Humpty Dumpty back together again." Only our loving and powerful God can do that, and, yes, He uses His Word of truth in Scripture to bring the wounded to Jesus where real healing occurs.

The second university campus was the Naval Postgraduate School, Monterey, California, long regarded as "The Annapolis of the West," because as its name implies, postgraduate education in the sciences of conducting war, as well as peace, were the academic emphases. The "cream of the officer crop" from the Navy, Air Force, Marine Corps, Army, Coast Guard, and officers from the military of foreign nations, came to one of the most beautiful educational settings in the world.

Most of the American students had come from sea duty, over-seas duty, or unaccompanied duty. Assignment to the postgraduate school was regarded by in-coming students and their families as a time for some relaxation as well as learning. This myth was soon dispelled by academic demands, which laid pressure upon students and their families. The Navy wasn't about to provide a "county club" environment as a reward for duty spent at sea or overseas away from the family. A common saying in the postgraduate student community over many years was: "Three things can happen. You will either get a divorce, have a baby, or buy a dog." Intensity in academia was a reality in Monterey.

In this setting from 1975 to 1978, I served as senior chaplain. I was blessed to have a chaplain representing the Roman Catholic Church as my co-worker in ministry. The biggest difference for me between the two campuses was support personnel. At USIU, I had a "lone-ranger" ministry, only in the sense that God used me as His witness. At Naval Postgraduate School, I had a Christian support team made up of countless witnesses who believed that Scripture is the Word of God. Campus Crusade for Christ, with Chuck Price at the helm, Officers Christian Fellowship, The Navigators, and scripturally committed students and their wives supported the Protestant Chapel program, which I believe at that time, was the Navy's strongest Protestant chapel program.

The program had to be strong because there was a continual revolving door of students whose stay in Monterey varied from eighteen months to three years, depending on the field of study. The student body numbered twelve hundred plus. I don't know of a civilian church that has to face a population upheaval like that.

The focus of the overwhelming majority of the students was on their careers. They were the front runners in a king-of-the-mountain environment, which prevails in the officer communities they represented. They were hard-chargers, focused on their mission, and most susceptible to tunnel vision. God and family, while important, didn't quite supplant the career drive. As such, many came to Monterey in a spiritually bankrupt condition. They had been tainted and influenced by the secular world, which placed great emphasis for success on diligent hard work. Many looked to themselves as their own personal career saviors. Naval Postgraduate School was viewed as a stepping stone, a launching pad to career enhancement.

Suddenly, at Monterey, the bottom dropped out. Academic pressures, coupled with family conflicts, mounted in leaps and bounds. Abruptly, their king-of-the-mountain positions began to crumble and they reached for help. My office was a continuous activity of spiritual counseling in God's Word, and the power of that Word took hold in lives that had been spiritually barren. Suddenly, dormant spiritual lives came to life in Jesus and in His Word. They drank thirstily of God's Word and came to a living faith in Jesus as their Lord and Savior. Many brought their wives into contact with our numerous Bible studies, and God's Holy Spirit worked new life in them.

It was not the chaplain doing the witnessing by himself. As noted above, it was the entire chapel team, living their faith in Jesus and in His Word that was contagious. Christian students sent their fellow students and their wives to my office, or witnessed to them and invited them to Bible studies and occasions of Christian fellowship, which abounded to God's glory in Monterey. New lives for old unfolded by the power of God's Holy Word; and then God sent them to duty stations and ships all over the world. His witness was multiplied by a degree known only by God.

I would like to have remained at the Naval Postgraduate School the rest of my Navy career, but as the disciples learned in the Transfiguration of our Lord, there was a time for a mountain-top experience, and a time to descend into the valleys of every day life. The Navy made that more than evident in its continual rotation by orders every two or three years, in order to meet the demands of sea duty rotation, a most humanitarian act. Otherwise, orders to sea duty would have meant a career spent in a ship or ships that spent weeks and months at sea in endless rotation between the home port and wherever the Navy had need on or underneath the sea. Retention of personnel would have been a critical issue.

Nevertheless, my three blessed years of ministry at Naval Postgraduate School, Monterey, California, stand in second place to my Vietnam ministry where my ministry was always to those who might or were about to die in battle. To this day, I can not go to the Vietnam Memorial Wall in Washington, DC. The pain is too much. I vividly remember battle and its sounds, the dead and the memorial services for the dead with bayoneted rifles stuck in the red earth of Vietnam, helmets on the rifles and the sound of "Taps." In that setting, our God planted me to preach His Word of Life and

Truth. Some of my Mt. Airy classmates, who vehemently opposed the war in Vietnam, labeled me as one who gave aid and comfort to "killers in uniform," and they severed our relationship. I have reached out to them, but their silence continues.

Above me as I write, is a painting by Lee Teter entitled *Reflections*. In it, a Vietnam veteran in civilian clothes stands with his right hand on the Vietnam Memorial Wall. Within the wall, as on the other side of a glass partition, stand Army, Navy, Coast Guard, Air Force, and Marine Corps dead who reach out for the hand of the living person touching the wall. *Refections* hits the guts of those who were there and who came out alive, though scarred, just like those from World War I, II, and Korea. Had there been no war ministry, peacetime ministry in Monterey would have jumped to the zenith of what any clergy person, committed to Scripture as the Word of God, could ever experience in uniform or out of uniform. It was God's Word in full-blown power!

I began this chapter with a brief summary of the confusion and deception of some theologians, past and present, regarding Holy Scripture as truly being the Word of God. In king-of-the-mountain moves, they tried to out-muscle God and His Word either by claiming superior scholarly authority, so as to sit in judgment on God's Word, or abandon it to the riptides of secular accommodation in theology. I have ended the chapter with my personal witness that Scripture is the Word of God, both in campus situations, and in the combat hell of Vietnam. I have seen its power bring people to faith in Jesus, Who makes new lives out of old lives. God's Word, in witnessing to Jesus as Lord, is the answer to the secularism of spiritual death that we see all around us, and yes, maybe within our own lives.

God's Word in all its fullness points to Jesus Christ as Lord. He alone, is the Savior of your life and mine. Holy Scripture, in all that it contains, proclaims the majesty and glory of God. And from that glory radiates a love for you and me, God's beloved; a love that was incarnated in His Son for our salvation and God's beloved in the world. Why, oh why would any scholar or scholars want to taint such love or thwart God's purposes in His Word, when it is God's beloved who are the ones confused and deceived by their "enlightened" conclusions concerning His Word?

Biblical scholars do not have to play "King of the Mountain." Our God doesn't play games with His Word! His beloved, we the people of God, mean everything to Him. . . even the giving of the life of His Son, given for you and me on Calvary's Cross. Jesus is the center of Holy Scripture. He reveals in His life and death, the very heart of God. Can there ever be a more blessed message for you and me?

Notes

1. John Macquarrie, *20th Century Religious Thought,* (Philadelphia: SCM Press, London, and Trinity Press International, second impression, 1989), 447.
2. News release, *Reporter, The Lutheran Church-Missouri Synod,* St. Louis, Missouri, November 1993, 1.
3. Ibid., 4.
4. David F. Wells, *No Place For Truth,* op. cit., 175.
5. Ted Peters, *GOD-The World's Future,* (Minneapolis: Fortress Press, 1992), 4–5.
6. Ibid., 5.
7. David F. Wells, *God In The Wasteland,* (Grand Rapids: William B. Eeerdmans Publishing Company, and Leicester, England: InterVarsity Press, 1994), 131–132.
8. Louis A. Smith, *State of The Church Reports, Lutheran Forum,* vol. 30, no.1 (Delhi, NewYork: The American Lutheran Publicity Bureau, February 1996), 40.

Chapter 13

More Consequences

The words of the Lord are pure words; As silver tried in a furnace on the earth, refined seven times. (Ps. 12:6)

Some consequences of questioning Scripture as the Word of God, which impact upon the Christian church, and upon the world to whom it ministers, have been addressed in preceding chapters. We share and bear these consequences. We stand at the end of a pipeline of history, which pours out its blessings, as well as its curses. Indeed, because we are in both church and world, whether we acknowledge it or not, we are participators in history as well as recipients.

As a flavor of the theology and philosophy that has been shaped by the Enlightenment, I have highlighted the assaults upon God's Word in Scripture by some representative scholars of those disciplines. I believe that what influences and affects the church's way of interpreting Scripture, impacts upon the spiritual lives of the people of the world to whom God's message in His Word is addressed. Suffice it to say the assaults are related to *confusion* and *deception,* words that have laced this presentation. These consequences are not only the work of the devil; they are his greatest joy.

When you and I venture out into the world of ideas and theories today, we are like the family that goes to the beach for a refreshing swim and a picnic involving fun and good food. Once we are settled with our beach blankets and our beach territory is established, something strikes our ear and catches our attention. All around us are other beach-goers on blankets, with boom boxes blaring rock music from different stations. The refreshing noise of the surf, as well as our conversation, is zeroed out. We find ourselves in a noise vacuum, sealed off from our family members. We are alone in a crowd of noise.

Ideas and theories bombard us in machine gun fashion! They become like the cacophony, the harsh, discordant sounds of rock music. Confusion rises to the level of normalcy, where being alone in a crowd of noise or world of ideas is common place. This can be seen in the bombardment of Internet data wherein any theory or idea advanced has equal weight as "being true, or partially true." Identical with this mix is an authority of the twentieth, and now in the new millennium of the twenty-first, century of confused thought called *inclusiveness*.

Inclusiveness demands that truth must encompass all the theories of man on any given subject, whether theological or otherwise. Nothing must be excluded or denied. The theory of inclusiveness attempts to bring all ideas together, so that hopefully a synthesis can be obtained and labeled as truth, a meltdown of God's absolutes. In the post-modern world, this is viewed as "trying to get at the truth," a slippery and unfulfillable goal. God, however, is not a God of wishy-washy synthesis. He is a God of absolute truth in His Word. The living of that truth, by the faith God supplies, is the "proof of the pudding."

In summary to this point, I have described the attack by theologians and philosophers on the transcendence of God, beginning in Chapter 6. The holiness of God in all His love actions in creation and in history and His message of truth in Holy Scripture have been targets of opportunity. This has evolved into a subjective dominance of what man interprets as truth or posits—declares as truth—by his own authority over and against any objective truth from God in Scripture.

Thus, to attack God in His transcendence is to reduce the objective, absolute truth of His Word to a subjective review and to judgment of His Word by man. And by the way, this opens the floodgates so that anything about Jesus, His Incarnation as well as His Resurrection, is wide open for judgment by the jury of man. This jury is made up too often of proponents of the historical-critical method, who have attracted a liberal audience of followers in academic positions in the seminaries of our nation. What flows from the seminaries, flows into the churches of America. And you, the people of God, are the recipients.

To affirm Scripture as the Word of God and confess that Holy Scripture declares absolutes of truth, the authentic message of God to His beloved people, is to be a bigot, a right-wing religious nut, devoid of sympathy and consideration for the right of man to be his own definer of truth. This is the assessment of the liberal left in theology upon the conservative right. Politics can not claim exclusive rights to those terms in which the extremes are emphasized. Conservative Christians hold to an *exclusive* view of Scripture wherein Scripture is the inerrant and infallible Word of God. Liberals and even some moderates hold to an *inclusive* view of Scripture wherein the theories of scholars are raised to a level of authority that can attempt to discredit Scripture as the true Word of God. No theory of man that questions Scripture can be excluded. All must be rolled together as "credible" considerations for modern minds to ponder. Confusion and deception mounts.

Another reality in our world today that confronts the Christian church, is the consequence of *relativism,* the heart of post-modernism. It is the cousin, the off-shoot of subjectivism and inclusiveness. Once truth is made relative, the definer becomes the power figure of authority. In my Navy days in Washington, where I was the pressure point of the Navy Chaplain Corps in defining the needs of the Corps for ministry in the Naval Establishment, (both Navy and Marine Corps), I quickly learned that the *one who defines* is the power person.

If you are not defining, you are not in the ball game. The crunch, however, comes when there is more than one person or entity making the definition. The clash in the power struggle to be the definitive authority soon dissipates in compromise, so that all theories are relative, in that there are no absolutes. Compromise may be the way budgets are finally established and laws made, but compromise has no place when confronted by the absolutes of God in Holy Scripture.

Without absolutes from God, what do we have? We have preaching wherein the Word of God comes as a mystery, devoid of God's absolute truth, relying upon the wisdom of man to re-interpret God's Word, in a relativistic way, for modern mankind in predicaments never before encountered by the God who created him. It is this "never before predicament" scenario that energizes the theological thrusts of today. Whether it is the causes of racial equality, feminism, the justice of liberation, or pro-death (as in abortion and euthanasia) to name a few, the Word of God stripped of its authority to address, has about as much power as a wet noodle. When God and His Word are believed to be manageable by man, we have views and options being expressed much like the rock-music cacophony of the beach scene previously described.

A classic example comes from a liberal Anglican publication, *The Witness*. In this publication, a book review is given by Harvey H. Guthrie, Jr., Dean of the Episcopal Divinity School in Cambridge, Massachusetts, who is now retired. He reviewed the book, *Skeptic in the House of God,* which was written by James L. Kelly in 1997. It is an account of Mr. Kelly's fifteen years as a member of St. Mark's Episcopal Church, Washington, D.C. In those fifteen years, he acknowledges his membership in that church, while serving as a full participant in the life of the congregation, editor of the parish paper, elected vestry member, and Sunday School teacher. In the review, Mr. Kelly was pictured as "an unrepentant skeptic with regard to the existence of God."

What really captures interest in this skeptic, who denies the existence of God, is the response of the rector of St. Mark's Episcopal Church, the Rev. James Adams, to Kelly's position of skepticism.

> Kelly's rector at St. Mark's, Jim Adams, has it right in explaining why there is no common doctrinal core at St. Mark's or in the Episcopal Church: '"What you have instead is a common core of practice. You can form a church around orthopraxy (Right action or practice, my insertion). . . . Our practice is very conservative—in our services from *The Book of Common Prayer,* in our organization. . . . The Episcopal Church going back for centuries, is more interested in orthopraxy than in orthodoxy. Anglicans have never been able to agree with each other on doctrine. And that's why I feel at home in the Anglican tradition."[1]

If the ELCA would "feel at home" with the above definition of Anglican tradition, and many Anglicans do not, are they ready to embrace "full communion" with the Episcopal Church in the name of ecumenism? This issue is still being addressed and debated. Could it come down to a relativistic dismissal of scriptural absolutes regarding doctrine in favor of what man defines as conditions for unity? I raise these questions because, whether in the present or future tense, they will surface as dominant issues in American church life. Ecumenism is a movement, dominated by a majority of liberal denominations, who embrace the historical-critical method, and who want to pull under "one roof" the churches of Christendom, because they assert they have more that binds and unites them together, than separates them.

Relativism, regarding what a denomination is willing to surrender as non-essential to its biblical foundation—its confession of faith, is the issue as it redefines Scripture. Unfortunately, ecumenism means compromise of doctrine, which Holy Scripture establishes, and this is another of the consequences when Scripture is not held to be the authentic Word of God. Compromise of doctrine means deception and confusion for the people of God.

In June of 1992, at St. Olaf College in Northfield, Minnesota, ELCA bishops, clergy, and laity came together for Call To Faithfulness II. Paul R. Hinlicky, editor of *Lutheran Forum* commented, *"The dissent between participants in Call to Faithfulness II is about a common perception of theological incompetence, if not a drift to apostasy, at the heart of the ELCA's life"*.[2]

Lutheran Forum printed the keynote address given by Carl E. Braaten in which he severely criticized what was happening in the ELCA. Here was a leading theologian of the ELCA taking his church to task. It also printed a response to Braaten by Walter Sundberg, a faculty member of Luther Northwestern Theological Seminary in St. Paul, Minnesota, and also of the ELCA. What is interesting to note is that he does not deny what Braaten described in his address as a troubled state of the ELCA.

After you read the following quote, please ask these questions: Would these conditions exist in a Lutheran Church that holds to Scripture as the infallible and inerrant Word of God to which the Lutheran Confessions stand as faithful witnesses? Can these conditions of a troubled state in the ELCA be attributed to their hermeneutical marriage with the historical-critical method of biblical interpretation? Sundberg wrote:

> Carl Braaten invites us to consider the troubled state of the Evangelical Lutheran Church in America. In his view, the difficulties of the fledgling denomination are not to be solved by fund-raising, reorganizing, or task forces. Rather, he says, we face a "spiritual battle," "a struggle for the soul of the church." Braaten offers a sobering list of problems that are symptomatic of the church's condition: the assault upon biblical language and tradition by the demand for inclusive language; politicization of the church's bureaucracy and programming; the dominating influence of psychology and sociology on theological method; the uncritical acceptance of scientific naturalism and subjective humanism; a misdirected spirituality that indiscriminately divinizes world, self, and even folk spirits; an allegiance to a type of historical criticism that divorces itself from "the faith once delivered to the saints" (Jude 3).
>
> These are just some of the problems that we have encountered as a new church these last five years. Braaten is not interested in trying to deal with them one by one. He has a larger concern. He contends that we face not only a host

> of specific problems, but that we are in danger as a Christian community. We are losing our faith in the God of the scriptures and the tradition of the church.[3]

Could the enemy of darkness and confusion have written a more devastating scenario for a church in infancy? The above appraisal by ELCA theologians does not, by any means, assert that ELCA has all the problems and that the LCMS is spotless and clean, all problems solved. But the above does give evidence to what can happen when the Enlightenment "virus" of the historical-critical method creeps in and infects the theology of a church and passes on consequences of that "virus" to the people of God in confusion and deception.

It is because denominations, churches like the LCMS, stand firm and tall against compromising Scripture as the Word of God—the absolute eternal message of God to His beloved—that they are attacked. If you don't know it by now, please know this: the devil doesn't deal in absolutes, unless they are absolutes of *his* making. If you don't see or believe that an attack against the very foundations of God—Father, Son, and Holy Spirit—and His Word has been launched and is on-going by those of liberal theology, then you may be like a Frenchman who thought that what was going on in Normandy on 6 June 1944, was a show of fireworks, a premature celebration of the French Revolution.

Relativism, where values are redefined, questioned, and too often rejected; where being subjective and not objective is "where it's at;" and where God and His Word are consigned to the dungeon of obscurity, real consequences fall on the people of God. Has the historical-critical method of biblical interpretation been a player in this mess of confusion? Of course it has. While not fully culpable, it has aided and abetted such issues of conflict and confusion as abortion, euthanasia, crises in human sexuality, and the disintegration of the family as a cohesive order of God's creation.

This is quite an indictment. However, when authority is questioned or taken away from God's Word in Scripture, the people who are affected by such action are like a ship at sea that has lost its compass. Loss of direction equals confusion. It can also mean physical as well as spiritual death. The abandonment of Scripture as God's inerrant and infallible Word fits that confusion and chaos scenario regarding authority. When our God and His Word are not in control, who is? And if you are taking time to come up with an answer because you are unsure of your answer, it may be that you are thinking *subjectively* and not *objectively*. This is the way post-modernism influences our lives. It takes our eyes and hearts away from Jesus and Scripture. It focuses attention of mind and heart upon what we want, what we want to define as truth, because we have been led to believe that we can have the final word. If the truth of God is "up for grabs," so that relativism reigns, the outcome is deception and confusion, and God's people take it on the chin once more. The prince of darkness laughs and dances with glee.

The consequences of inclusiveness and relativism in regard to abortion as mentioned above must be seen in the light of God's Word, which is most clear in regard to life in the womb. Psalm 139:13–18 declares:

> For Thou didst form my inward parts; Thou didst weave me in my mother's womb. I will give thanks to Thee, for I am fearfully and wonderfully made. Wonderful are thy works. And my soul knows it very well. My frame was not hidden from Thee, When I was made in secret, And skillfully wrought in the depths of the earth. Thine eyes have seen my unformed substance; And in Thy book they

> were all written, The days that were ordained for me, When as yet there was not one of them. How precious also are Thy thoughts of me, O God! How vast is the sum of them! If I should count them, they would outnumber the sand. When I awake, I am still with Thee.

Other Scripture passages which bear upon this most important subject of life are: Genesis 2:7, Psalm 127:3, Isaiah 49:1, Jeremiah 1:5, and Luke 1:44, to name a few. The consequence of abortion is death, and whenever the starch is taken out of the authority of God's Word, not only confusion, but death, does occur.

Auschwitz, Dachau, and other Nazi concentration camps of World War II, will never top the death toll of innocent children murdered by abortions, occurring daily in America since 1963 when the Roe vs. Wade court decision became accommodating law for post-modernism. I firmly believe, that had the Christian churches of America been committed to Scripture as the Word of God, millions of children would not have died by choice, and abortion would be "made rare." Roe vs. Wade would be in legal text books as failed litigation and not as a "green light" for the killing of unwanted children in the womb or partially out of the womb.

Dr. John M. Swomley, Emeritus Professor of Ethics, St. Paul School of Theology, Kansas City, Missouri, in *The Human Quest,* a journal for the religious liberal, presented a liberal view of fetal life in the womb. He used the term "fetal idolatry" in regard to the position of those opposed to abortion. In his position of total disagreement with the sanctity of life in God's Word, he wrote:

> OPPONENTS OF ABORTION in America have attributed to fetal life a sacredness that is actually idolatry. The idol in Old Testament terms was inanimate, made of metal or stone. As such it was possible to attribute to it a

> tribe's cultural or group interests and to worship it instead of God. Idolatry is therefore the absolutizing of a cultural belief system as if it is sacred or of divine origin and therefore more important than human personality; it is something to which sacrifice must be offered.
>
> Fetal idolatry denies a woman's right to control her body, her life, her destiny, all of which must be sacrificed to an embryo or fetus once she is pregnant.[4]

Another illustrative consequence of abortion, rarely mentioned, is post-abortion syndrome. It can hit a woman years after the abortion. Its criteria is identical to the post-traumatic war syndrome experienced by combat veterans like myself. When the reality hits concerning what abortion has done to her child in the womb, a woman can frequently be swept by guilt and regret into the depths of depression. If per chance, the reader has experienced, or is now experiencing post-abortion syndrome, seek the counsel of your pastor, who, hopefully, is committed to Scripture as the Word of God. As well, find a crisis pregnancy center that will work with your pastor or priest in the healing process. My beloved, Barbe, has been a post-abortion group facilitator since 1981, and has seen healing take place, but only in and through God's Word, in all its totality, as it points to Jesus Christ as the Healer.

Denominations that espouse the pro-choice line of unscriptural conclusions, have been co- contributors in the deaths of children, the number known only to God. Christian clergy and their influenced laity who embrace the historical-critical method have laid a plowed garden ready for the seeds of abortion to be sown. Clergy who are in churches where the sanctity of life is held in the totality of scriptural truth, and who are timid for fear of losing members and financial support, and who fail to witness to their people in the full strength of God's Word on this subject, are also co-contributors of death.

What pertains to abortion, also pertains to euthanasia, man standing as the judge of life and death. This stance is made easier when man can stand as judge over the Word of God and have the "last word," so that he can come to a finality in thinking, but not in reality. God not only has the first word, He has the last word. The other way around is deception, confusion, and death.

The consequences that may impact the reader the most reside in the family arena. Not all families have been confronted by the abortion issue (which certainly is growing in America's families), but all of us have been affected. However, we can not escape the sexual revolution that has erupted in America and which has grave consequences for the family.

As a parish pastor and a Navy chaplain, I have been in the midst of the issues of family life where abuses in human sexuality too often have been a dominant theme. The American family has been caught in a sexual cacophony, the discord of thought and ideas regarding human sexuality. *Playboy* magazine and its philosophy splashed upon the American scene in the early 1950s and was taken by sinful human beings as truth. It was followed by *Hustler* and *Penthouse* magazines, which further sanctioned that sex has no boundaries. The American family was invaded by a new pseudo-truth, the absolute of the unrestrained, unrestricted libido. Unrestrained sexuality became the norm, as another relativistic, unscriptural conclusion, the exploits of which, have become a reoccurring theme for R- and X-rated movies and television series and finally, an accepted way of life.

David F. Wells, in making the point that people today turn more to their bodies than to their psyches, wrote:

> One quite predictable turn in this regard is a revival of the worship of sexuality. For example, Carter Heyward, an Episcopalian theology professor, speaks of sexual experience as "sexual godding." In an epigrammatic chapter heading, she cites a theological student's testimony that one "of my most profound experiences of Goddess is with my lover—while we are having sex and especially at the moment of peaking, I feel a deep sense of her love and presence with me." This is deified experience. It is a substitute for the genuine article.[5]

The deification of sex has left the family in confusion and chaos. Sexual permissiveness has promoted the spread of sexually transmitted diseases such as aids, chlamydia, genital herpes, gonorrhea, syphilis, and other venereal diseases. Sex out of bounds in marriage, has greatly contributed to the soaring divorce rate in America.

When denominations, which cling to the historical-critical method of biblical interpretation, sanction masturbation as healthy, homosexual unions as normal, approve same sex marriages as condoned by God, teach teens how to use condoms, and ordain homosexuals and lesbians for the office of Christian ministry, they have abandoned the authority of Holy Scripture for all of life. They are co-contributors to the confusion that is, sadly, alive in God's people. What a contrast is embedded in God's Word in 1 Corinthians 6: 9–20.

This confusion, which is not to God's glory or honor, is a confusion that leads to spiritual death. The people of God have "taken it right on the button." The family unit has been assaulted in much the same manner as God's Word has been maligned. The family, as one of God's order in His creation, has been cast aside and has been raped by "new ideas and theories," which arise apart from the truthfulness of God's

Word in Scripture. These ideas and theories are spawned in post-modern swamps of decadence, swamps of deception and confusion.

In the ships where I served as chaplain, if the navigator was "off" by one degree of the compass, we would never have arrived at our destination. One degree of deviation multiplied by the miles we sailed from Hawaii would have put us hundreds of miles from Subic Bay in the Phillippines, which was our destination before we headed to the Tonkin Gulf in support of Seventh Fleet operations.

Just to be "off" in direction by one little degree of the compass could result in lostness and possibly death, if we wandered into a deadly typhoon that suddenly changed direction, and from which we could not escape. This happened to Navy ships as World War II was drawing to an end in the Pacific, and it could be the explanation of the famous mystery of the "Bermuda Triangle" in the Atlantic Ocean where ships and airplanes suddenly disappeared.

Like the compass in a Navy ship, God's Word sets the direction of God's truth. Thus, hermeneutics, which questions God's Word as truth, causes a course deviation in truth from God's Word to man's word, which results in confusion and spiritual death. Lostness in everyday living and spiritual death are not possible options but sudden realities called "unintended consequences." Unintended consequences such as those listed above can happen and do happen. There are always consequences when the authority of God's Word is questioned and discarded.

Other consequences can be named, but one that is often ignored is the trust factor of God to speak truth in His Word. We know that Jesus never questioned or criticized the Old Testament. He completely trusted it as the Word of God. Therefore, when human scholars question Scripture as the true Word of God, they are attacking the trust factor of God's Word. If God can not be trusted, who can be trusted? The consequences are obvious evidence of a lack of trust, as well as lack of respect for authority—whether it is God's authority in His Word, which is the authority of the Christian church to preach and teach with power, or the authority of the state as one of God's orders of creation to preserve peace and freedom for its people.

If an opinion poll were to be taken today, asking if trust can be held in God, the Bible, the church, or the state, I would venture to predict that the results would indicate by an overwhelming majority that trust can not be conferred on any of them. We live in a "trust-less" society where attacks against God, His Word, His Church, and His creation of the state raise questions that create doubt and confusion. Of course, the sinfulness of man in both church and state has to be addressed. However, it is the orders of God's creation, in which the family is included, that are buffeted and assaulted by the swirling winds of distrust. The orders of God's creation have long been held to be: the state, the church, and the family. All three have been victims of the Enlightenment and the historical-critical method.

You and I live in the world where those consequences break upon our lives like waves upon the shore, never ceasing. In light of those consequences, may our God open our eyes and hearts to see why His Son came to earth as Redeemer-Lord. The spiritually wounded and dying are all around us; yes, maybe even within our own families. What opportunities we have to share with them the power of God's Word, the Gospel of Jesus, in the full context of Holy Scripture.

God doesn't leave us speechless or without a love mission. As Jimmy Valvano, the renowned basketball coach at North Carolina State, said as he was dying from cancer, "Don't give up! No, never give up!" He wasn't talking merely about winning basketball games. He was talking about the living of this earthly life. We who know the Master and the truthfulness of His Word know about a life beyond this life on earth. In the faith that the Holy Spirit provides, we can trust God for life with Him here on earth and forever. It is this truth which must be proclaimed, and one which we can never compromise or give-up; no, never give up, not for ourselves, nor for God's wounded beloved.

Why? Because our God has declared it so in His Holy Word, the Scriptures! Just read, believe, and see how God works the truth of His Word in Scripture. You will come alive in Him, an aliveness to life here today and forever, an aliveness in God's Holy Spirit that not even the most gifted pulpit orator could ever express. It already has been given and stated in God's Holy Word. God and His Word are *alive!*

Notes

1. Harvey H. Guthrie, Jr., review of "Skeptics in the House of God," by James L. Kelly, *The Witness*, vol.8, no. 4, (Detroit: April 1998), 26.

2. Paul R. Hinlicky, editorial comment in Lutheran Forum, *The American Lutheran Publicity Bureau,* vol.26, no.2, (Delhi. N.Y.: Advent 1992), 3.

3. Ibid., 11.

4. John M. Swomley, "Idolizing The Fetus," *The Human Quest,* (May–June 1998), 12.

5. David F. Wells, *God in the Wasteland,* op. cit., p. 52. (The Anglican professor referred to in the quote is the same Rev. Carter Heywood quoted in the media as well as on the Michael Medved radio show of 21 January 1999 when she said: "I'd rather go to hell with Bill Clinton than to beat down the gates of heaven with Ken Starr.")

CHAPTER 14

Blessing & Honor
Honor & Blessing

But He said, "On the contrary, blessed are those who hear the Word of God, and observe it." (Luke 11:28)

A decision to change church membership (and in my case church endorsement) so I could continue in ministry in the United States Navy, was not a casual decision. It entailed long hours of prayer, asking God for direction. Would He have me leave the LCA, or would He have me remain in that church and stand tall as a witness for Him and His Holy Word?

For years, I witnessed to clergy and laity of the LCA that our church was on a course that did not honor Scripture as the Word of God. I was witnessing to those who were fully entrenched in the historical-critical method. No doubt, there was the question in their minds, "How can anyone educated at Mt. Airy not be on board regarding the historical-critical method?" Mt. Airy is the popular name given to the Lutheran Theological Seminary at Philadelphia, because the seminary is located in the Mt. Airy section of that city.

The genesis or the beginning of my decision to leave the LCA was sown in an initial encounter with a professor at Mt. Airy, to whom I referred in Chapter 5, where the words, "We are going to do away with your Sunday School faith and build you into a mature faith," resonated upon my heart and ears. The negation of the Christian nurture in the Word of God that I had received in my home and in my church created a question mark that lasted throughout my seminary years.

Was I to abandon the spiritual "roots" from which I came? Was God's call to be a pastor now different from what I had anticipated? As a neophyte seminarian, I was confused and in wonderment. As I wrote in Chapter 5, "Wow! Was I now being privy to some sort of spiritual blessing because I was within the hallowed walls and halls of seminary? Was this seminary experience going to give me a higher level of understanding what faith is about? Was I about to stand closer to God than I had ever stood before?"

What a way to begin a seminary education! In that confused state, I tried to assimilate what the curriculum infused into my academic life. I read and studied theologians who were committed to the historical-critical method, and confusion reigned. Why? Because it was foreign to my belief that Scripture was and is the Word of God. To say that I didn't question myself would not be accurate.

Certainly, the academic brilliance of my professors had an influence on me. However, there was always a nagging reservation of doubt that maybe I was the one who was woefully out of step. When I studied God's Word in devotions and in preparation for field work assignments of preaching and teaching, always before me was the absolute authority of Scripture, which I could not deny, and which was in open conflict with the historical-critical method, the method of hermeneutics at Mt. Airy Seminary. Confused? Of course I was!

I remember sharing with my parents the doubts I had about the way the Word of God was presented and how "out of step" I felt in the whole process. Their counsel to me was to continue seminary education, knowing that there was graduation and ordination ahead of me. Then, I would be a pastor who could preach God's inerrant and infallible Word to God's people. This seemed to be the only way for me at that time because the LCA was the only Lutheran church I knew and the LCMS was portrayed by my professors as "not quite with it . . . exclusive . . . separatistic . . . and not where a true Lutheran should be."

I pressed on. I put my head down, much like a fullback rushing for a first down with a yard to go, and I pushed onward. Perhaps, at the end of my academic experience, there would be an enlightenment reality that would trump my confusion, declaring that my confusion was of my own making and that I was the guilty one. Therefore, in repentance, I would cease questioning my Mt. Airy experience. I confess I was almost there. To deny that would be untruthful. Yes, I had studied on my own that the Scriptures were and are the Word of God, but now the seminary which would certify me for ordination, and the national church which would ordain me to the Christian ministry, were not of that belief. Was I in a dilemma? Of course I was!

A requirement for ordination by the LCA was subscription to the historic Lutheran Confessions as true expositions of God's Word in Scripture. In my mind were questions: How can this requirement be fulfilled if Scripture is not the Word of God in every respect because it only contains the Word of God? Is the LCA doing "an end-run" around the Confessions?

Dr. Theodore Tappert, one of the renowned confessional scholars of Lutheranism, explained to our class that we could make subscription to the Confessions *in so far as* they were true. He showed our class that we didn't have to subscribe *because* they are true. He pointed to history when the Lutheran Confessions were written. He maintained that the issues then encountered and the alternatives that were then offered were right for that time. Thus, a conditional subscription could be given. I went along with the class and was ordained. Years later, as I was in ministry, I realized my subscription to the Confessions was a compromise. It is *because* they are true expositions of Scripture, that they are valid for all time. A conditional, historical method of interpreting them because they may be "out of step" for today, cheapens and confuses the Confessions and God's Word with which they agree. More about the Lutheran Confessions will be discussed in the next chapter.

I believe that my preaching and teaching, while in the ULCA and the LCA, honored Scripture as the true Word of God, inerrant and infallible. An exciting example of the power of God's Word in God's people occurred at St. John's Evangelical Lutheran Church, Hatboro, Pennsylvania. I was called as pastor of that congregation in April, 1956. I remained until called to ministry in the chaplaincy of the United States Navy in June, 1965. When I arrived at St. John's, the membership was just over 300 confirmed members. When I preached my last sermon in St. John's Church, confirming 60 youth as adult members of the church on Pentecost, 6 June 1965, the adult confirmed membership stood above 1200. In nine years of ministry at St. John's Church, growth mounted by 100 adults per year. In 1965, our Sunday school enrollment totaled 850 children.

Did I display a magnetic personality? No! Did I do anything out of the ordinary to cause such growth to God's glory? No! I just knocked on countless doors and I pray, simply ministered as a faithful servant of the Word, proclaiming God's Word in all its power. God's Holy Spirit did the work. I am not that gifted or smart. To God be the glory! It was not until the eighth or ninth revision of this book that I was led by God to include the above. I chose to include it as an example of God's inerrant and infallible Word at work in the hearts and lives of His beloved. God has all the power and all the glory, and His people have His blessing of life in Jesus, to which the Scriptures testify truthfully and with the super-abundance of God's power.

My discomfort with the LCA grew as I saw the church turn its face away from the sanctity of life in the womb and embrace a pro-choice stance. This I could not sanction. In addition, I saw the church falling head over heels in love with social issues where words such as, *peace, justice, liberation, solidarity, empowerment, women, social change,* and *vital urgency* highlighted the mission of the church. The greatest discomfort, however, was the LCA's position on the Word of God. (A contemporary summation of that position was given by Beverly J. Stratton in Chapter 11.)

A presentation by the Rev. Will L. Herzfeld on the subject of Liberation theology solidified my discomfort and heightened my frustration with the LCA. This presentation was given at the January 1983 Lutheran Chaplains Convocation in Coronado, California. At that time, chaplains representing the LCA, the LCMS, the ALC, and the AELC, came together for meetings with their church-endorsing agents and for study of a theological subject, given in alternate years by a scholar of a representative church.

Rev. Herzfeld was a bishop of the AELC. As he unfolded his initial day's presentation, it was obvious to many chaplains that what we were receiving was a Marxist presentation of Liberation theology, with a contortion of Holy Scripture woven throughout. It was oppressive to me, as it was, once more, a liberal slant away from Holy Scripture as the Word of God. It could only be a product of the historical-critical method. There before my eyes and ears was the epitome of what the LCA was becoming as it moved toward a possible merger with the ALC and the AELC. I spent at least an hour in prayer that night asking God to show me where He wanted me to be, in ministry within, or outside, the LCA.

The next morning we learned that Rev. Herzfeld was called home to Oakland when his wife developed a sudden illness. The convocation fell flat as Liberation theology was not on the front burners of our theological expertise. Time was wide open for discussion. I sought out a dear chaplain friend, Jim Shaw, who served as the senior Army chaplain at Ford Ord, not far from the Naval Postgraduate School in Monterey. We had many memorable hours of friendship in each other's quarters, and it was only natural that Jim and I should talk. At this time, Jim had retired from the Army and was the endorsing agent for the LCMS. I poured out to Jim my theological frustrations with the LCA and with Herzfeld's presentation. He listened as a friend, but gave no counsel.

As I had many friends in the LCMS at that time, I was impressed with their reactions to what Rev. Herzfeld had presented, for their reactions were my reactions. My brothers in the LCA, on the other hand, did not voice to me any semblance of displeasure regarding the theology presented. It was business as usual.

I returned to duty in Hawaii and throughout the Pacific Ocean area where I served as Force Chaplain, Fleet Marine Force, Pacific (FMFPAC). My prayers intensified that God would show me His will for the expression of my ministry. Should I remain in the LCA, or should I leave? I found myself occupied with this prayer request. The many hours I spent in airplanes flying across the Pacific Ocean between Hawaii and Japan, and between Hawaii and the mainland of the United States, were hours of looking at my ministry with the question: Can I faithfully represent the LCA as one of its chaplains?

Tension mounted in my heart. My prayers of many years, intensified even more as I asked and pleaded with God to reveal His will to me. I knew I could not place God in my employ, but I also knew, in faith, that He would give me an answer. I did not want to take any action on the authority of my own reason. Had I consulted Holy Scripture? Of course I had, and what I read in God's Word was an authority which the church I represented did not hold as sacred. Yet, God laid upon my heart that I should persist in prayer, and the prayers went on.

The LCA was my church, and I prayed for it to be free of the historical-critical method. I had a bond with my church and my brother clergy. At times, I could be in disagreement with them over theological issues. It isn't unusual for Lutherans to be in disagreement. But to be in disagreement over the meaning of the Word of God was a crucial issue. I prayed and hoped that the LCA would come back to their confessional roots wherein Holy Scripture is honored and blessed as the Word of God, and not merely the receptacle that contains the Word of God.

The answer to my prayers came at 0400 on 19 May 1983, when I was awakened and heard these words: "I will bless what I can honor. I will honor what I can bless." I sat up in bed. I wasn't dreaming. My whole being shook. My ears heard these words which were spoken with authority. These words came to me one day shy of the twenty-ninth anniversary of my ordination.

I believe these words came as an answer to prayer. Skeptics may say that I was dreaming and that God doesn't work that way today. I know otherwise. I was wide awake. I woke Barbe, my wife, and told her what happened and the words I heard, "I will bless what I can honor. I will honor what I can bless." Together we prayed a prayer of thanksgiving, that our God had heard our prayers, for Barbe was and is my prayer partner.

I know that God's revelation in His Son and in His Holy Word is all the revelation a Christian needs. I subscribe fully to that truth. Yet, the words I heard were not, I believe, words of the devil, for the words pointed to God's Word and a course correction (good Navy words) for my life in terms of my relationship to the LCA. I believe I had the answer to months and years of prayer regarding where God wanted me to do ministry in His Name, according to His Word.

Without a doubt, I believe it was God, through His Holy Spirit, speaking to me. I believe God speaks through His Spirit wherever and whenever His Holy Word is the issue and when He has opened a heart to faith. The timing is always His. It was not an extra revelatory happening apart from the Holy Scriptures. I believe it was a revelation in accord with His Holy Word. I believe our God will bless what He can honor and He will honor what He can bless. If that is not in accord with His love action in Jesus, I do not know what is. To my God is all the glory and my thanksgiving. In Chapters 16 and 17, I will point to the power of the Holy Spirit in regard to His written Word, the Holy Scriptures.

Any doubt or confusion as to my course of action was dispelled. I had to leave the church which raised me, ordained me, and which I had served for over twenty-nine years. I could no longer serve a church that did not honor the inerrant and infallible Word of God, and so bless its people with the truth and power of that Word. I had to free my ministry of any connection with a church committed to the historical-critical method, a method that does not honor and bless the Word of God, but allows man to stand as its judge and jury.

In the months following my 19 May answer to prayer, I was in contact with Jim Shaw, and ultimately, with

Dr. Robert Sauer, first vice-president of the LCMS and Dr. Arnold Kuntz, president of the Southern California District, LCMS. It was suggested that I look at Missouri for a year and that Missouri look at me for that same time in a colloquy process wherein I would spend time at an LCMS seminary. I chose the seminary at Fort Wayne, Indiana, the same seminary that my son, Eric, chose to continue his seminary education prior to ordination for ministry in the LCMS. At my own expense, while on leave from the Navy, I was there for three weeks in the summer of 1984. Dr. Samuel H. Nafzger, executive secretary of the Commission on Theology and Church Relations, LCMS, taught the class I selected, Lutheran Hermeneutics, and so wetted my appetite that this book would eventually be written.

Almost simultaneously, God led me and my son, Eric, to the LCMS. We had shared with each other our frustrations regarding where the LCA was heading, especially in its embrace of the historical-critical method. Eric was enrolled at the Lutheran Theological Seminary, Berkeley, California. When I called him from Hawaii and told him what I held to be God's direction for me, he said, "Know what, Dad? I came to that conclusion some time ago. I, too, have to leave the LCA. I was about to call and talk it over with you." Talk about God's timing! The Holy Spirit is active in the "moving business."

By September 1983, Eric was enrolled at Concordia Theological Seminary, Fort Wayne, Indiana, where both he and I found a joy and an excitement in being with brothers who held Scripture as God's inerrant and infallible Word. While both of us came to our conclusion independent of each other, we walked away from the LCA's confusion and deception surrounding God's Word, into a radiance of love for God's Word and the theology of the Cross that flows from God's Word, the Gospel of Jesus Christ, in *all* of Scripture. Their theology has been, and is, liberal; while the theology of the LCMS, tied to Scripture as God's inerrant and infallible Word, is conservative. It boils down to the matter of presuppositions about the Word of God, which I discussed in Chapter 3.

My colloquy process was completed by July of 1985 when I was received into the ministerium of the LCMS. It was two plus years of preparation, regarding which, Dr. Robert Preus wrote to me in a 29 July 1985 letter, the following: "I am only sorry you couldn't get into our Synod a little quicker, but I think nothing was harmed by the delay. Needless to say, I am delighted that you are a member of our ministerium." My brother in Christ, Jim Shaw, was understanding, helpful, and always Christ-centered in God's Word. I was blessed to have had him where God had placed him at a time in my life when I needed a "confessional" friend who understood where God was leading me.

While the process of moving from one church body to another was ongoing, I didn't want any fuss to be made concerning it. I wanted to keep it quiet for the reason that at that time, I was either the first or second in rank seniority of all Navy Lutheran chaplains on active duty. To me, it was a private, spiritual decision that I didn't want to escalate into a Chaplain Corps/ Lutheran debate, which could have easily happened, if I had not opted for the way I chose.

Thankfully, the LCA understood, although they would have preferred my change of churches to have occurred at the time of my Navy retirement. I could not accept that delay, for I was at the point where I could no longer represent the LCA as one in harmony with their theological position regarding the Word of God and the theological implications flowing from that position. Once God released me to make the change, I had no other alternative.

I can be criticized in many ways for not leaving earlier. I accept any and all criticisms. One thing I know. I sought my Lord's leading in prayer over the years, and until He released me, as I believe He did in the words: "I will bless what I can honor. I will honor what I can bless," only then was I able to leave the LCA. How I longed for my church to abandon the historical-critical method of biblical interpretation. It did not.

I held out as long as I could as a witness, until, I believe, God indicated otherwise and moved me to a church where Scripture is regarded as the inerrant and infallible Word of God. This is a blessing, where ministering to God's people is with authority and power, which Holy Scripture declares as the true Word of God. I believe that when the authority and power of God's Word is preached and lived to God's people, they are the blessed ones, and who in turn, honor God and His Church in its love mission of the Gospel proclamation to the world.

As I look back over my years of parish and chaplain ministry representing the ULCA and the LCA, before it became the ELCA, I did not encounter any serious questioning by my contemporary pastor/chaplain friends regarding the direction of the church. The historical-critical method of biblical interpretation was well in place, social issues were in the cross-sights, and pro-choice was considered the "right" choice.

I am sure there were dissidents upon the scene, but in the years spent in chaplain ministry, I was not involved in what the civilian clergy and laity were writing or saying about the LCA. My ministry was focused upon my Navy ministry, especially to those who had been involved in the Vietnam War and its aftermath impact upon their lives and the lives of their families. I had little time to be "up to date" concerning what was happening in the LCA. This changed when the merger of the LCA, the ALC, and the AELC became a possibility.

As the new church was being formed, all sorts of questions and criticisms surfaced. What I read caused me to ask, "Isn't this the predicted result of a church committed to the historical-critical method?" I was able, I believe, to see the problem, but I thought I could be an effective chaplain in ministry in spite of the theological stance of the church I represented. I was wrong. God had to bring to my ministry a "course correction."

Recently I read the words of two clergy of the ELCA who may possibly stand where I stood some years ago. They stand as representatives of pastors deeply concerned about the direction of their church. I suspect they also hope and pray for a course correction. First, the Rev. David A. Gustafson, pastor of Peace Lutheran Church, Poplar, Wisconsin, in *LOGIA*, wrote about the past, present, and future of the ELCA. The following are some quotes from his article:

> Questions regarding the use of inclusive language caused controversy. For example, the use by some of "Creator, Redeemer, and Sanctifier" as the baptismal formula became such an object of concern that the Conference of Bishops released a statement upholding the traditional formula of "Father, Son, and Holy Spirit." Another more recent controversy developed over the first draft of the "Statement On Human Sexuality," which advocated recognition of committed homosexual relationships and allowing homosexual unions. These examples illustrate the theological confusion that is present in the ELCA. Gerhard Forde, professor at Luther Seminary and a member of the CNLC (Commission for a New Lutheran Church, my insertion), sounded the alarm during the course of the CNLC's deliberations. At one point he observed, "Nowhere in the documents do we hear the word 'catholicity' to describe ourselves, only 'inclusiveness.'" Forde proved to be right; inclusiveness replaced catholicity as the defining mark of

> the church—the result being that, in the instances cited above, fidelity to the Scriptures and the tradition of the church (creeds, confessions, liturgy) has been threatened or simply ignored.
>
> Concerns for the ELCA's future have been expressed in many quarters; however, the most pointed expression of those concerns was presented in a document issued on the Feast of the Annunciation of Our Lord, March 25, 1995. It was entitled *9.5 Theses Concerning the Confession of the Faith in the Evangelical Lutheran Church in America* and was initially signed by eight pastors from New Jersey. Its message was straightforward and to the point: "The ELCA is in a crisis—a crisis of faith. The critical question is whether the church will prove faithful to the prophetic and apostolic Scriptures and the catholic creeds and evangelical confessions, or fall into apostasy—a fall which could go either to the right or to the left."[1]

Gustafson also wrote about the failure of the ELCA to deal with seminary curricula.

> Over the years, requirements in the core disciplines of Bible, church history, and theology were reduced as sociological and psychological courses were added, either in the form of requirements or as electives. This can only result in seminary graduates having less knowledge of the Scriptures and the tradition and a diminished (or confused) consciousness of what it means to be a pastor. If the church does not deal with this matter, Lutheran identity will be threatened, and the ELCA will experience the theological erosion that is so characteristic of American Protestantism.[2]

The second ELCA pastor, the Rev. Leonard R. Klein, pastor of Christ Lutheran Church, York, Pennsylvania, wrote in the "Letters" section of *Lutheran Partners,* the following in response to a previous letter in that publication:

> Many of us, however, believe that much of what is happening in the ELCA is beyond acceptable diversity and cannot be dismissed so easily. The slogan of "inclusiveness" has led the ELCA into advancing and entertaining options that many consider at odds with the faith and morals of the one holy, catholic, and apostolic church.
>
> Structurally and ideologically, the ELCA was set to head out on the fast track to becoming a mainline liberal American denomination. This has led to a diversity that violates our confessional and biblical foundations. Accordingly, the ELCA is beset with conflict on a wide range of volatile issues—ecumenical arrangements that seem inconsistent with the Lutheran confessions, homosexuality and abortion, even the language for God.[3]

The above comments ultimately go back to the hermeneutical roots of Scripture. When those roots are not firmly fixed and growing in Scripture as the inerrant and infallible Word of God, there is the absence of a norm—an authoritative standard—and the results are inevitable. The bottom line is, our God will not bless what He cannot honor and He will not honor what He cannot bless. Can it be any other way?

Notes

1. David A. Gustafson, "The ELCA: Its Past, Present, and Future," *LOGIA*, vol.V, no.2, (Plymouth, Minnesota: Eastertide, 1996), 41–44.

2. Ibid.

3. Leonard R. Klein, *Lutheran Partners,* Letters Section, July/August 1998, p. 7.

Chapter 15

Word of God and the Lutheran Confessions

You search the Scriptures, because you think in them you have eternal life; and it is these that bear witness of Me. (John 5:39)

Lutheran churches of the world honor statements of doctrinal confession, which are contained in the Book of Concord, known as the Confessions. However, it must be noted that the Confessions are not subscribed to, or given the same level of trust, by all Lutheran churches. As was described in the last chapter, ordination in Lutheran churches involves a personal subscription to the Confessions. It is the acceptance of scriptural articles of faith, doctrine, and practice, which are in harmony—in agreement with—Scripture.

Unfortunately, subscription varies among Lutherans. It runs the gamut of subscription *because* the Confessions are true expositions of Scripture, to merely, *in so far as* they are truthful expositions of Scripture. The former is the position of the LCMS, while the latter is the position held by the ELCA. The ELCA's position is based on limiting the Confessions historically, in that they applied fully to the time and age in which they were written, but are not completely applicable today. The influence of the historical-critical method is in evidence here. The LCMS maintains that the Confessions—like Scripture—are not limited by time. They are true expositions of Scripture. Their truth is not conditional.

"Symbols" is another term used for the Confessions and is synonymous with the word "confession." The Symbols are confessions of the faith, or doctrine, of the Lutheran Church. Lutherans are familiar with portions of the Confessions in the Book of Concord. The Apostles' Creed and Nicene Creed are confessions of faith used in worship, along with an occasional use of the Creed of Athanasius, all three being part of the Confessions of Lutheran churches. Teens and adults, prior to being accepted by confession of faith in confirmation or baptism into membership in the church, study *Martin Luther's Small Catechism,* also a part of the Lutheran Confessions.

The best description of the Book of Concord, which is stated in a clear and understandable presentation, comes from Robert D. Preus in his book, *Getting into The Theology Of Concord.*

> This *Book of Concord* contains a quite divergent assortment of creeds and formal confessions which however have one thing in common, a doctrinal unity, a united commitment to the teaching of the Gospel of Christ. In this book are the ecumenical creeds, developed and written from the second to the sixth century, long before the Reformation. Included also are Luther's Small Catechism

and his Large Catechism (1529), which were not originally intended to be confessions at all in the usual sense, but were written for children and ordinary adults to summarize the Christian faith and the way of salvation for them. Perhaps the most important confession included in our *Book of Concord* is the Augsburg Confession (1530), written by Philip Melanchthon and presented on behalf of the Lutheran princes of the day at a very important meeting with the emperor to testify to the world exactly what the Protestant churches in their lands taught about the Christian religion and the Gospel. A year later (1531) Melanchthon wrote a defense of this great doctrine called the Apology of the Augsburg Confession, a very lengthy treatise in which he defends the theology of the Augsburg Confession, especially on such crucial issues of the Reformation as justification by faith, the importance of good works, the work of Christ, repentance, and the like. In 1537 Luther was asked to write a confession for a church council the pope suggested he might hold but which never came about. It was written in a little town called Smalcald and is called the Smalcald Articles. It is a bold and militant document, but at the same time exhibits Luther's great heart and concern for the Gospel and for the church, and it wins the reader by its sincerity and conviction. Later in the same year Melanchthon wrote a short Treatise on the Power and Primacy of the pope because Luther had seemingly not said enough about this in his Smalcald Articles. This too was included in our *Book of Concord*. After Luther died, all kinds of controversies and misunderstandings broke out among the Lutherans in Germany. After years of debate and monumental attempts at settling the doctrinal issues the Formula of Concord was written in 1577. This was a joint undertaking of a great many Lutheran theologians who wanted only to settle the dispute and remain

> faithful to their Lutheran heritage. They were eminently successful. The Formula of Concord was signed by thousands of Lutheran pastors in the German empire; at a later date the Lutheran Church in Sweden and in Hungary also signed this document. Now peace (concordia) was established. The Reformation and the cause of the Gospel went on, uninhibited by doctrinal controversy. In 1580 all these creeds and confessions were incorporated into the Book of Concord, which Lutheran pastors subscribe and to which they pledge themselves today.[1]

As stated above, the Confessions are expositions of Scripture. They do not stand in the same authority as Scripture because they are not divinely inspired but are doctrinal explanations of belief and practice, founded upon the teaching of Scripture, the absolute norm of faith. The Confessions are secondary norms, in that their entire intent and content must be in harmony with that which Scripture proclaims and teaches as God's truth.

James W. Voelz, in his book, *What Does This Mean?* defined the nature and function of confessional statements.

> A confession speaks about the Word of God Incarnate (Christ) in harmony with the words of God incarnated (sacred Scripture). And so, in its innermost nature, a confession restates what has been heard and received by the confessor, whether that be an individual or the church. A confession repeats what God says, and, as such, it is a speaking that is congruent with sacred Scriptures which are God's Word. . . . To say that a confession is congruent does not mean that it either simply parrots or repristinates but rather that its content corresponds to the content of Scripture and in no way does violence to the total thought.[2]

Dr. Carl Ferdinand Wilhelm Walther, the founding theologian and first president of the LCMS, in a synodical essay written in 1884, held Scripture as the sole norm, judge, and source of doctrine. His main point in the essay was to show that articles of faith and doctrine must be based on the foundation of Scripture and not on the writings of the church fathers, even though those writings are held as treasures. His words, which follow, show the place of the Lutheran Confessions in honoring the exclusive authority of Scripture as it witnesses to, and proclaims Jesus as Lord:

> It was a chief tenet of the church of the Reformation to base articles of faith, not on the writings of the fathers, but only on the Holy Scriptures. In the *Smalcald Articles* we read: "God's Word shall establish articles of faith, no one else, not even an angel" (SA II ii 15). We read further in the *Formula of Concord,* "we also pledge ourselves to the first unaltered Augsburg Confession, not because it was written by our theologians, but because it is taken from God's Word, and is well and firmly founded in it."(FC SD Sum. Form. 5) We do not hold the Augsburg Confession, the foundational confession of our Church, to be such an important document, to which we subscribe with joy, because it was authored by such highly enlightened men, but because it is in such precise agreement with God's Word.
>
> Luther expresses himself regarding the correct attitude of a Lutheran toward him and his writings, in the following manner: "There are many who believe on my account, but they alone are the real believers, who remain (in the teaching) even if they should hear that I myself (which may God forbid) have apostatized and fallen away. . . . For

> they do not believe on Luther, but on Christ himself." (WA 15, 1988 f.)[3]

What Dr. Walther pointed to was one of the three fundamental doctrines of Lutheran theology that comes from the Word of God. We saw the emphasis of *sola Scriptura,* Scripture alone, meaning that Scripture is the only norm of Christian doctrine. This is the position of the Confessions. *Sola* is the Latin word meaning "alone." The other doctrines, *sola gratia* and *sola fide,* by grace alone and by faith alone, are faithful expositions of Scripture about justification. Martin Luther focused upon justification. It was the central doctrine of all his writings. Lucidly, he defined justification for the lay person as follows:

> By the one solid rock which we call the doctrine *(locum)* of justification we mean that we are redeemed from sin, death, and the devil and are made partakers of life eternal, not by ourselves . . . but by the help from without *(alienum auxilium),* by the only-begotten Son of God, Jesus Christ.[4]

Sola gratia, by grace alone, points to God's righteousness as God's free gift, the source of justification. Grace does not come from man or through man, but from God alone, *sola gratia. Sola fide,* by faith alone, is the only way man can receive God's grace, and this faith is a gift from God wherein justification is received *sola fide,* by faith alone. Faith, a gift of God's grace, trusts God for His mercy and grace in His Son and in His Word. Life with God, is wrapped up in justification by God's grace alone through faith alone—God's free gifts—for Christ's sake, which must always be seen as God's work in and for us through the power of God: Father, Son, and Holy Spirit. *Sola Scriptura, sola gratia,* and *sola fide,* point and witness to Jesus, our

Lord and Savior. Read Romans, chapters 3–5; Ephesians 2:8,9; and Philippians 3: 8,9 as examples of Scripture's declarations in regard to justification, the central doctrine of Christianity. The Confessions faithfully witness to that doctrinal position.

The United States Navy has an order that the captain of the ship or the officer having the "conn" (having control of the ship's movements) executes, depending upon situation and circumstances, which is, "Steady as you go!" This is an order to the helmsman to mark the ship's heading by degrees at the moment of the order and return to that heading, and steer that course. Believe me, it avoids many collisions at sea and inevitable death and destruction.

The Confessions are just that. They "steer the course" of doctrine which comes from, and is in accord with, the Scriptures. They are the course heading of any church committed to Scripture as the Word of God, and they gladly proclaim and confess what Scripture decrees. The Confessions never dispute or question God's Word. They honor and bless God's Word as His saving truth, which points to Jesus as mankind's Savior from the sin, death, and confusion of this world. "Steady as you go!" is their hallmark of truth, founded in God's Word. The people of God in churches steering that course are blessed. They are blessed with life here on earth and life with Him forever, as God intended.

In the Navy, we have a term of affirmation that is positive and good for the ship and its crew. It is a response by one in command, to a positive suggestion by a junior officer or enlisted member of the crew. "Make it so!" affirms positives, and that is what the Confessions do. They affirm the positives and validity of God's Word as inerrant and infallible in the doctrine they promulgate.

Just as the ships of our Navy have to steer away from collision, which compromises the ships' ability to function and survive, so Christian churches have to "steer the course" of faithfulness to God's Word. But have they? You, the reader, are left with that decision. Has your church been "confessional," meaning faithful in proclaiming and teaching the Word of God, or has the *word of man* replaced scriptural authority? You may be Lutheran, Methodist, Presbyterian, Disciples of Christ, United Church of Christ, or of another denomination, but the ultimate question facing you concerns faithfulness to God's Word in Scripture. Does your church proclaim with might and dignity the truth of God in His Word, or has that truth been bent by this world's teachings in compromise to the truth of God in favor of the truth of man?

Are you hearing and being taught something that does not coincide with God's Word? Indeed, is God's Word in Scripture now obsolete and out of date? Have man's theories, wobbly though they are, attained the stature of true authority, and so subrogate (substitute) man's feeble mind, for the loving and truthful mind and message of God in His Son to His beloved? You, dear child of God, can find yourself standing in one of three possible positions in regard to God's Word.

First, the prince of darkness would have you stand in confusion, unsure of your God and of His Word in Scripture, and perhaps unsure of your salvation. Second, human scholars committed to the historical-critical method, would have you believe that not all of Scripture is the Word of God, that Scripture only *contains the Word of God,* and is not *the* Word of God throughout, and needs correction or revision to meet post-modern spiritual needs. Third, the way of scriptural truth—the way God's Word directs, blesses, and honors! It stands upon the holiness of our God Who speaks through His Word. It is God speaking His message in inerrant and infallible words, the only way our God chooses to speak, which is in accord with the majesty and glory of all that He is. This is something we mortals can not comprehend here on earth, but look forward to when our God, in Jesus, will come again, as Holy Scripture promises.

An unfortunate reality in some Christian churches today is the uncertainty of its members regarding what the Scriptures teach and proclaim. Knowledge of God's Word and the doctrines of scriptural truth that flow from that Word, the Gospel of Jesus, are not "hot" issues today. That doesn't mean they won't be. This is a result of the "greased pig" of pulpit proclamation, which is not in accord with the Word of God. It leaves the person in the pew questioning their very salvation.

That doesn't mean these churches will always preach the "other gospel." In my own denomination of the LCMS, the error of holding Scripture in low regard, as the historical-critical method does, was overturned—largely by the laity. I believe the time is coming when His infallible and inerrant Word in Scripture will be embraced by some churches now committed to the historical-critical method.

In the meantime, faithfulness to His Word in Scripture, and the doctrine that flows from Scripture (which proclaims Jesus as Lord and Savior), must be the confessional practice of those in love with Jesus and in love with those who have yet to come to faith in Him by the power of the Holy Spirit. It means, as well, that those of us who hold in faith the Scriptures as the Word of God, must witness to our neighbors and to our world, that Jesus is Lord and Savior as His Word attests. A head and heart knowledge of Jesus, by itself, will not work.

From the head and the heart must come mouth, hands, and feet witness of Jesus as Lord and Savior. All that we are must be God's communication channel for His Word in us to His beloved, who as yet do not know or love Him. This is also the purpose of the Confessions—to proclaim and teach Jesus—in accord with Scripture.

Those who wrote the Lutheran Confessions in the sixteenth century wanted "to steer the course" of the church's confession for all time until Jesus returns. In the face of heresies and assaults upon Scripture, they wanted Scripture to be clear and understandable, by the power of God's Holy Spirit, to the common man for salvation. It is as simple as that.

Yes, these writers had to stand tall for Scripture as the Word of God against the ecclesiastical forces that questioned the Confessions' declarations as true exposition of God's Word. The Confessions were not written as an ecclesiastical hobby by theologians with plenty of time on their hands. They were in battle for the truth of God's Word for God's beloved people. Salvation of souls was the issue. Therefore, when you read the Confessions, you encounter not only affirmations concerning God's truth in Scripture, but also condemnations against positions and theories, which were not, and to this day, are not, in harmony with Scripture. Not to do so would have been what we call in the Navy and Marine Corps, dereliction of duty. Not only that, but they would have been unfaithful to God's Word. That charge can not be leveled against the writers of the Lutheran Confessions.

Yes, the Confessions were written in an age of theological conflict, and that age of conflict has yet to go away. The main hermeneutical question still upon the theological horizon is, "Can Holy Scripture be equated as Word of God?" It is a question of authority. Does God still speak His Word in all of Holy Scripture, or are there parts of Scripture that are not the Word of God? Therefore, does Scripture merely contain the Word of God, as a glass contains water? How full is the glass? Is it overflowing or almost empty? When scholars tinker with and question the Word of God in Scripture, they assume the authority that the God of the Scriptures alone can claim.

The same applies to the Confessions. Either the Confessions witness to the authority of Scripture as the Word of God from which they are its exposition, a witness—not an authority—or something else must be placed as the authority of the Confessions. When the Confessions can no longer be held as expositions, in that they repeat what God says, they must be downplayed to the same extent that Scripture is downplayed as merely "containing" the Word of God. In any church that subscribes to the historical-critical method, the Confessions take on that lesser character. They may stand as a reference, but a reference that can be altered or changed according to man's scholarly findings, and, as such, lose their authority of witness as truthful expositions of God's Word.

Mark this well, for this is a hermeneutical issue which brings more clearly into focus what Johann Salomo Semler of the eighteenth century maintained, as discussed in Chapter 7: "The root of evil (in theology) is the interchangeable use of the terms 'Scripture' and 'Word of God.'" You will recall that Semler did not accept using these terms as equals, since he maintained that not all of Scripture was the Word of God. He placed a divide, or a wedge, between Scripture and the Word of God and was then free to be the authority in determining what could or could not be the Word of God in Scripture.

It is not surprising or strange that this same emphasis of Semler has emerged on the confessional scene since the historical-critical method was embraced first in liberal European theological seminaries in the nineteenth century, and later in liberal American seminaries early in the twentieth century. It impacted the LCMS at Concordia Seminary, St. Louis, where it reached epidemic proportions and was finally purged and discarded in the first half of the 1970s.[5]

Authority for a liberal church, like the ELCA, when confronting the Confessions, is the Gospel. They hold the Gospel to be the defining doctrine in the Confessions. An orthodox church like the LCMS will never discount or devalue the Gospel as the message of God in Jesus Christ for salvation. Yet, when the Gospel is elevated as the supreme authority for the Confessions, something has been drastically left out, omitted—namely, the Holy Scriptures, which proclaim the Gospel. Something else has also been omitted. It is the Law.

In Chapter 4, it was stated that the Law of God in Scripture convicts us of our sinful nature, while the Gospel proclaims what Jesus has done to save sinners like us from eternal death and damnation. Unless we are convicted by the Law, we have no need for the Gospel and the Gospel is weakened. Both Law and Gospel must be observed, and this is exactly what the Holy Scriptures uphold. Both are different doctrines. While the Law must function, it dare not take precedence over the Gospel, which is the proclamation of what Jesus has accomplished for our salvation from sin and death, that which the Law could not accomplish. The Law never saves. It condemns. It shows us our need for the Gospel. A proper distinction between the two doctrines must be maintained, but both are needed. One or the other dare not be ignored, or else we have a Scripture which is not of God.[6]

A truthful and realistic relationship between Scripture and Gospel is given in the Study Edition of *A Statement of Scriptural and Confessional Principles*, published in 1972 by the LCMS. It highlights that which the Confessions assert.

> The Gospel, which is the center of our theology, is the Gospel to which the *Scriptures* bear witness, while the Scriptures from which we derive our theology direct us steadfastly to the *Gospel* of Jesus Christ.[7]

To emphasize the Gospel at the expense of the totality of Scripture, is to deny the full picture of God's revelation in His Word. Dr. Robert D. Preus has written the following in regard to the Gospel standing as the norm for Christian doctrine:

> . . . the implication . . . is that the authority of Scripture is nothing but the power of the Gospel it proclaims.
>
> Now, such a position utterly confuses the function of the Gospel with one of the functions of Scripture. It confuses the power of the Gospel with the authority of Scripture. And thus it undermines both.
>
> Scripture is the authority for the Gospel according to our Lutheran Confessions . . . The infallible authority of Scripture does not diminish the wonderful and saving power of the Gospel, but supports it. And the power of the Gospel does not vitiate the divine authority of Scripture. Let us leave the Gospel its power—not only when we may read it in Scripture, but wherever it is preached and taught in the church. And let us leave Scripture its authority.
>
> Then, we will not only be talking sense, but we will be talking like confessional Lutherans.[8]

When the Gospel stands as the norm for Christian doctrine above and beyond the Holy Scriptures, which proclaim the Gospel, the result is called "Gospel reductionism." This clearly and boldly is a theological attempt to elevate the Gospel, while at the same time, criticizing and undermining its scriptural foundation in God's Word. In terms that the lay person may not have heard, it is the assertion that there is a canon within the canon, a subject that will be discussed later in this chapter.

When the Gospel is taken out of its God-given foundation, the Holy Scriptures, and called the norm for doctrine, any course can be steered, because the Gospel can be allied to any wind blowing across the theological tundra, free from the obstruction and constraints of Scripture, free to roam, free to define, free to confuse, free just to be free. This is because it has been cut loose from its authority, the Scriptures. Then, when Feminist theology tries to change God's revelation in Scripture; when Liberation theology tries to become the focus, the praxis, the action of theology; and when inclusiveness becomes a virtue and orthodoxy a sin, so that Jesus Christ is one of many ways to salvation, we can see first hand how the Gospel can be bent and contorted. Its very foundation is separated from the foundation of the Holy Scriptures.

Underlying all the above is the historical-critical method wherein man sits in judgment upon the Word of God. To sit in judgment really means that one has authority. So if man has the authority over God's Word in Scripture, he can define whatever he pleases and even make the Gospel a vehicle of his own definition. Then, the Gospel can be attached to any movement upon the social scene as the impetus and the cause of praxis or action. Not only is God's authority in His Word compromised, but God in Christ is diminished and viewed as being in the employ of man, the definer. This is completely foreign to the proclamation of the Lutheran Confessions as true exposition of the Word of God wherein *God is the definer* of His grace in Jesus Christ.

Another feature often ignored in the relationship of Holy Scripture to the Confessions or the Symbols, is the tendency and temptation of modern scholars to go beyond the Confessions and establish as believable fact, new creeds and confessions. Carl E. Braaten wrote in the ELCA's textbook on Dogmatics (dogmatics is a branch of theology which seeks to interpret the dogmas or teachings of a religious faith):

> The confessional life and understanding of the church need not be static. The church is free to take the risk of extending the confessional limits of her own tradition. The confessions are not the final formulation of the Gospel. New confessions will need to be written and subscribed from time to time. The past creeds and confessions of the church must not be glorified, for the church is made up of sinners on their pilgrim way, possessing at best imperfect and fragmentary knowledge.[9]

The proposition in the above quote can not happen in a church fully committed to Scripture as the Word of God and the Confessions as faithful expositions of that Word. Any change would have to be within the parameters of Holy Scripture, which would make the Confessions null and void. The Confessions have stood for centuries as truthful expositions of the Word of God.

A most important truth for the laity of our churches today, to comprehend and hold sacred, in order to rightly regard Holy Scripture and the Confessions, is the recognition of both the causative authority and normative authority of Scripture. The causative authority is simply the Holy Spirit Who works in and through the Scriptures and in the Sacraments to create faith in God's people. It is God's power in His Spirit that caused the Scriptures to be written. The normative authority of Scripture is the norm, the absolute standard our God has established for the proclamation, the witness of the Gospel. It is the divine arbiter between what is true and what is false. The causative and normative authority both emanate in God. These authorities which come from one authority, our God, are the issues which are disputed by the historical-critical method.

Martin Luther passionately held Scripture, the Word of God, as the foundation for all Christian doctrine. One of his famous quotes emphasizes what happens when compromise is attached to the Word of God, one of the devil's tactics of confusion and deception, a theme indigenous to this book:

> When the devil has persuaded us to surrender one article of faith to him, he has won; in effect he has all of them, and Christ has already lost. He can at will unsettle and take all others, for they are all intertwined and linked together like a golden chain so that if one link is broken, the entire chain is broken and can be pulled apart. There is no article which the devil cannot overthrow once he has succeeded in having reason dabble in doctrine and speculate about it. Reason knows how to turn and twist Scripture in masterly fashion into conformity with its views. This is very agreeable, like sweet poison.[10]

As promised, an explanation is needed to unravel the term "canon within the canon," a term that most of the laity of our churches probably have never heard. The word canon comes from a Greek word meaning "cane" or "measuring rod," something which measures. It came to be used in the scriptural sense as the final selection of books to be included in the Holy Scriptures that were recognized as *measuring up* to that which the Christian church held to be the genuine, inspired, original, and authoritative Word of God. Thus, the word "canon" took on the meaning of "rule," whereby the books we now know in the Bible have measured up to the *rule* as the authentic Word of God. They hold together as God's truth and mutually interpret one another. It was in the fourth century AD that the canon was firmly fixed as the authoritative Word of God. The *rule* was by the power of the Holy Spirit. No, never rule out our God working through His Holy Spirit. The power of the Word of God must always be seen as the power of God's Spirit, the Holy Spirit.

The thirty-nine books of the Old Testament and the twenty-seven books of the New Testament fall within the *rule*, the measure of being the Word of God. Therefore, to refer to the canon is to refer to Holy Scripture. They are identical and related.

For you, the laity of our churches, "canon in or within the canon" can be a confusing and deceptive assertion. You may have believed that all of Holy Scripture was and is the Word of God. What has happened that could cause you to change or question that belief? Once more it is the historical-critical method. Those who are the advocates of this method have tried with all their theological acumen, their adroitness of human scholarship, to make their case that all of Scripture is not the Word of God.

To make their case, they stand on the coattails of Johann Salomo Semler as their foundation, not on the inerrant and infallible Word of God. They say there is something within the Scriptures that they elevate as "the canon" within the original canon, and it is the Gospel. Therefore, the Gospel has the authority of being the true canon, the true rule, and it is the Gospel that is contained within the original canon that is the authority of the Bible. As I stated before, who can argue with or dispute the Gospel of Jesus Christ? No one! However, when the rest of Holy Scripture is abandoned as not needful or authoritative for the Gospel, something has happened. Holy Scripture is diminished and confusion and deception reign unbridled. I quote Braaten once more as he elucidates the position of the ELCA, a church in love with the historical-critical method.

> The Holy Scriptures are the source and norm of the knowledge of God's revelation which concerns the Christian faith. The ultimate authority of Christian theology is not the biblical canon as such, but the Gospel of Jesus Christ to which the Scriptures bear witness—the "canon within the canon." Jesus Christ himself is the Lord of the Scriptures, the source and scope of its authority.[11]

Certainly arguments can be made, but within the sphere of historical-criticism they come as arguments made to discredit Holy Scripture as being the Word of God. Please refer to Dr. Preus' comments (see Note 1) regarding Holy Scripture and the Gospel. His words do not dishonor Holy Scripture or the Gospel contained within. They do not abandon any part of Scripture. They confess and affirm that Holy Scripture and the Gospel are so intertwined that they contain God's love message to His beloved. They show as well, that there can not be a canon within the canon of Scripture. Any addition to add to the canonicity of Scripture, must be the addition of man's interpretations, in accord with the historical-critical method.

The confessors, in writing the Confessions, wanted the truth of God's Word in its totality to be proclaimed to God's people for their salvation. They wanted no clouds of uncertainty to raise doubt or unbelief in the lives of God's people. They wanted "to steer" the doctrinal course which the Holy Scriptures reveal as God's truth. And, yes, the Confessions do "steer the course" and they do "make it so!" so that doctrine coincides with that which the Scriptures proclaim and declare. In the final analysis, Scripture alone is the supreme authority. The Confessions never dispute that authority. Indeed, they testify to it!

Notes

1. Robert D. Preus, *Getting Into The Theology of Concord,* (St. Louis: Concordia Publishing House, 1977) 7–8.
2. James W. Voelz, *What Does This Mean?,* second ed., (St. Louis: Concordia Publishing House, 1997) 348–349. This work is recommended for the scholar who wants to dig deeper into biblical hermeneutics. My presentation, as I stated before, is for the lay people of God and does not attempt to approach the level of hermeneutical scholarship, which Voelz presents.
3. C. F. W. Walther, "Walther on Sola Scriptura," Walther's 1884 Synodical Conference Essay, trans. James Ware, *Concordia Journal,* (St. Louis, Oct. 1984) 372–373.
4. Martin Luther, *What Luther Says,* op. cit., vol. II, 701, #2186.
5. See Kurt E. Marquart, *Anatomy Of An Explosion,* (Grand Rapids: Baker Book House, Michigan, 1977), for an analysis of hermeneutical conflict in LCMS in early 1970s.
6. See C.F.W. Walther, *God's Yes and God's No*, (St. Louis: Concordia Publishing House, 1973) for a more complete distinction between Law and Gospel.
7. Study Edition of *A Statement of Scriptural and Confessional Principles*, Lutheran Church-Missouri Synod, 1972, 23.
8. Robert D. Preus, op. cit., 27–29.
9. Carl Braaten , *Christian Dogmatics*, op. cit., vol. 1, p.54.
10. Martin Luther, *What Luther Says*, op. cit., vol. III, 1165, #3729.
11. Carl Braaten, *Christian Dogmatics*, op. cit., vol.1, 61.

CHAPTER 16

The Laity and Holy Scripture, Connection Needed!

For whatever was written in earlier times was written for our instruction, that through perseverance and the encouragement of the Scriptures we might have hope. (Rom. 15:4)

Whenever anyone tries to make an interpretation, it is understood that a connection is essential. That which is interpreted must be made meaningful by the interpreter to the one receiving the interpretation. Otherwise, why try to make an interpretation? Biblical hermeneutics, which involves the interpretation of Scripture, has as its goal a connection between the canonical text of the sixty-six books it represents, and you. You, the reader with Bible in hand, can be directly connected by the power of the Holy Spirit. On the other hand, a church, a person, empowered by God, can bring a connection of God's Word to your life. Without a connection, hermeneutics would be an exercise in futility. Thus, biblical hermeneutics implies a connection between Holy Scripture and you, the child of God. One thing we can establish with certainty, the prince of darkness is only interested in a disconnect.

In previous chapters, I have given examples of hermeneutical interpretations. They have fallen mainly in the camp of those who espouse the historical-critical method as the correct way to make the connection between Scripture and you. You have tasted a flavor of the theologians and philosophers who have championed and helped to establish this method. As I have made clear before, my quarrel is with the historical-critical method.

The theologians I personally know, in academia and in the parish, who are committed to this method, are beautiful people of God. I know them from my previous years in the ULCA and the LCA. I prayerfully want them to see the Word of God in all its power and clarity. To be sure, there are some ELCA pastors who hold Scripture as the true Word of God and who have long abandoned the historical-critical method. They may be a vanishing breed because the pressure upon them from the national church is subtle and intense. Like a mighty theological giant, the ELCA has strong hermeneutical presuppositions, which radically differ from those who hold that Scripture is the inerrant and infallible Word of God.

I brought to your attention in Chapter 3 the fact that presuppositions are never neutral, and that presuppositions condition our connection to what is true and believable and what is not. Therefore, when an interpretation on any subject is made to us, it is received in the catcher's mitt of established preconditions of thought, that which we assume beforehand to be true or false. It is in this arena of thought contention and battle that interpretations are received or rejected. Either a connection is made, or it is discarded.

Many years ago, in Bloomsburg, Pennsylvania, my sister-in-law, Molly, was struggling with a washing machine.

She examined every feature of the washing machine over and over again and couldn't figure out why it would not work. She pushed the right buttons and checked the connection to the water supply, but nothing happened. It wasn't until my wife, Barbe, came upon her predicament that the problem was solved. Barbe put in the plug. Without a connection to power, electric washing machines simply do not work. For that matter, hardly anything else works without power, and that includes the Holy Scriptures of God. Power implies a connection, energy from its source to the user.

It is maintained that in the business world, having the "right connections" is essential for success. Yet, it is obvious that everything in life, in order to be meaningful, must have connections. God did not create us for isolation. The question is: "What are the right connections?" This is most definitely the prime question you and I face when interpreting Scripture or when it is interpreted to us. Is the connection from God, or is the connection from man, trying or attempting to supersede the authority of God?

In liberal churches, where the historical critical-method is embraced, the latter is the case. The pillar, upon which that method stands, presupposes that man has the authority to stand as the judge, the final arbiter, over Holy Scripture to make the connection.

When God's people are confused and deceived about Scripture being the Word of God, in that it only contains the Word of God, a wrong scriptural connection has been made. The power of the Scriptures, known as the Holy Spirit, has not been allowed to flow freely from Scripture to the child of God. The power has been compromised in the many attempts to make God's Word the word of man. Without the power of the Holy Spirit, all of Scripture makes no sense, and it is *all* of Scripture that God has given us. He has not divided His Word into two or more categories: the true, the false, and the inbetween.

I believe the right connection between God's Word in Scripture and your life and my life comes with proper "alinement." *Alinement* can also be spelled, *alignment*, the way most auto shops spell the word when referring to wheel alignment. I choose *alinement* for my purpose. It speaks of being in proper order, in the right relationship, in line, so that God's blessings and honor which flow from His Word, can be grasped and held in faith through the power of His Holy Spirit. God's line is a straight line in His Word. He never deviates from the truth that Jesus is our Lord and Savior. From Genesis to Revelation, the alinement comes alive in His Word, as He prepares rebellious and sinful man to be loved completely, to be redeemed completely, in His Son, Jesus. This is Gospel!

Why would theologians and philosophers ever try to subrogate (change) the Scriptures, which are in a straight line with the Gospel, so that some of Scripture is not Scripture? They must assert, then, that Scripture is out of "alinement" and crooked. A correction, by sinful man, must be made! Man will make it true and correct! He will wade through history and their documents, evaluate them—Scripture included—and arrive at conclusions, the conclusions of man. These conclusions will be promulgated as emancipated truth, separate from those who hold Scripture as Word of God and who are considered to be in the darkness and shackles of biblicism.

This emancipated truth brings with it deception and confusion. God's people don't know what to believe. Scripture has been called into question, and in its place are theories which "pull the plug" on God's Holy Spirit. Denominations in love with the historical-critical method are in turmoil. Membership losses continue to increase, financial support drops to basement level, and God's people lack any sense of authority they can hold onto with certainty. Then, liberal theologians and philosophers scratch their heads in despair and wonderment over what "the world is becoming," as though they never had any part in its making. It is their detachment from what they have helped create that amazes me, and at the same time, makes me weep. To present God's Word in the contorted theories of biblical scholarship (which the historical-critical method does) saps the power of God's Word. It is more than a short circuit. It is spiritual power failure for God's people who have been and are exposed to that method. It separates the people of God from the power of His inerrant and infallible Word. Such separation can lead to spiritual death. I can not even imagine the tears of God. Can God ever bless and honor what "enlightened scholars" have done to His Word and to His people?

Darrell Jodock, in his book, *The Church's Bible*, upheld the historical-critical method of biblical interpretation and presented the church as "*the community of faith*" (his words), as the authority for the interpretation of Scripture. In trying to dissolve scriptural authority as residing in the Word of God, and in reconstructing an integrated contemporary understanding of the Bible's authority as residing in the community of faith, he wrote:

> Scriptural authority is not foundational. . . . Far more important than specific teachings or beliefs *about* the Bible is an actual, active engagement with the Bible's contents and the claims it makes on the lives of persons in the community of faith. . . . A worked-out view is important in order to discern appropriate implications and explain them to others but is not required in order to make the Scriptures significant for Christian living. On the contrary, individuals or groups can experience the claim of the scriptural message without thinking through all the ramifications involved in their approach to the Bible; they need not, in this sense, possess any *theory* of

> biblical authority. If persons can find the Bible useful without having any theory of its authority, then surely agreement among Christians about a single theory is not necessary either.[1]

Jodock's aim was to bring:

> . . . a contextual interpretation of scriptural passages within the community of faith . . . toward a productive focus on the recontextualized meaning of texts.[2]

Recontextualization of Scripture is nothing more than the reconstruction of the authority of God's Word. Jodock placed the recontextualization within the post-modern setting. It was the historical-critical method being given full discretionary power to do with Scripture what a post-modern culture could accept. Central was the freedom, the assumed authority of the people of faith, to come up with their interpretation of the authority and meaning of Scripture. The power to connect the Word of God to peoples' lives was handed over to post-modern presuppositions. Any resemblance to Scripture being the authoritative Word of God was and is purely coincidental. It is clearly *the tail wagging the dog*! Jodock exemplifies the epitome of what is happening in liberal churches. He provided obvious clues in his view of the infallibility and inerrancy of Scripture. He maintained:

> Words like *infallible* and *inerrant* have been used correctly referring to inspired texts, but they are dangerously misleading in our own day. By calling too much attention to the scriptural words, they draw attention away from what the words are meant to point to. . . . scriptural infallibility lies in the Bible's failing in its proper

> task of pointing us in the right direction, toward revelation, toward the presence with us of the true God. . . . The terms *inerrant* and *infallible* are capable of misleading in yet another way. They obscure the need for ongoing reinterpretation.[3]

When God's Word is stripped of its inherent power and authority, and is judged to be less than what God has revealed it to be, it can be shaped like putty to resemble whatever a prevailing culture defines. Jodock's presupposition as to where biblical authority emanates, was most revealing.

> All theories of biblical authority involve extra biblical appeals to values or assumptions held by the prevailing culture. As the values and assumptions change from one cultural epoch to another, new or revised understandings of biblical authority are needed. It is necessary to take the cultural context seriously in developing, adopting, and using any theory of biblical authority.[4]

If you, the reader, are scratching your head in bewilderment over the above quotes, wondering how such conclusions about the authority of Scripture could ever have emerged, you are not alone. They represent a liberal development of hermeneutics, which has descended upon the Christian church since the Enlightenment, and which I have outlined in this book. Isn't this another example of subjectivity over objectivity in that the community of faith becomes the subjective authority for defining faith apart from the objective authority of the Word of God? This can be taken one step lower, so that the individual reader's perception or understanding of a biblical text, not the authority of the text itself, becomes the ultimate authority for the meaning of the text. This latter theory has been expounded upon by Edgar V. McKnight as a post-modern approach wherein the reader's orientation prevails according to which presuppositions are activated. Authority, then, is in the eye and heart of the reader. Post-modern relativism reigns supreme over God's Word in Scripture.[5]

Rudy Skogerboe, a urologist in Grand Forks, North Dakota, and a Lutheran layman, wrote a book entitled, *Who Has Stolen My Church?* He was aghast at what his church had become since World War II. The changes he saw and wrote about in his book are the changes that the lay persons in our churches have seen take place since the early 1950s. He wrote:

> Who, then, has stolen my church? Perhaps the church has not so much been stolen as it has been changed. In a way we all have stolen parts of the true church of Christ by choosing to compromise our beliefs.[6]

The examples I have cited from Jodock show a wide divergence, or gap, existing between what you, the lay person, were taught about the Word of God as a child or youth, and what you hear today coming from liberal churches. What Skogerboe wrote certainly pertains. Belief in the Bible as the true Word of God has been compromised! The authority connection of power between God and His Word in Scripture has been severely bent, and in some cases, severed.

Jodock is a product of the historical-critical method and, as a professor in a college with ties to the ELCA, has passed on and is passing on the presuppositions of that method to students who will be the leaders in our communities and churches in the new century. One final quote shows how the historical-critical method has attempted to rearrange the Word of God. After Jodock concluded that "Christendom has ended, . . ." he wrote:

> In the absence of any consensus regarding the concept of God, the believer is invited to participate in the construction or reconstruction of a doctrine that is more viable for postmodern, post-Holocaust times than classical theism is and more inclusive of the full range of biblical metaphors and images. The believer is not asked to accept a ready-made package but is called to participate actively and thoughtfully in the study and appropriation of Scripture and the insightful analysis of contemporary society.[7]

What he ignored, however, is the sinfulness of man in need of Jesus as his Savior. He allowed the sinfulness of man to play a defining role once he opened up any semblance of control of the Word of God to those who live in a sinful post-modern world. Once again, *it is the tail wagging the dog.* It is hermeneutics *out of alinement* with the Word of God. It is foreign to all that God's Word is and will always remain. Holy Scripture is His love message in Jesus, which comes through the inspiration of the Holy Spirit upon those He chose to write His revelation as inerrant and infallible truth.

You may hear and read the works of theologians committed to the historical-critical method, who will incessantly revile us who hold Scripture as the Word of God, as "out of date," as "in love with the Bible more than we are with Jesus," or as "the fundamental right-wing of Christianity." One thing that is not in short supply is the castigation of liberals upon conservative Christians who believe and live by Scripture as the inerrant and infallible Word of God. We are labeled as "crooked," " bent out of shape." I submit to you, in regard to the Word of God as His true Word for all time, who are the "crooked" in biblical hermeneutics today? Who wants to rob the authority of God in Scripture and return it to "the community of faith?" Formerly, it was a return to the enlightened minds of scholars, but when that faltered, an appeal to the broad spectrum of the community of faith was introduced.

Even the good-natured monks of St. John's Abbey in Minnesota have fallen prey to the temptation to reconstruct the Bible so that "a medieval Bible for modern times" might be published by 2004 in seven volumes. In it, they want "to create a Bible reflecting modern views of gender, culture, and ecumenicalism" in a 1,150 page Bible that "will be the first example of an illuminated, calligraphic Bible to be produced in the Western world in nearly 500 years." It will be known as the St. John's Bible.

Biblical reinterpretation is at the heart of this endeavor. In an attempt to downplay the reconstruction of Scripture, Brother Deitrich Reinhart, president of St. John's University, stated that it wasn't a New Age Bible, that it was deeply Christian—but deeply respectful of other traditions. The names of the ancestors of Jesus are written in Arabic as well as Hebrew and English to underscore the status of Islam as a kindred faith. Attempts to reach out to feminists, and to have some imagery from Hinduism, Buddhism, and even Native American shamanism are to be included "merely to shine light." "'We're not imposing messages onto the Bible,' the monk overseeing the project explained, 'but recognizing what is already there'".[8]

Donald Jackson, official calligrapher to the queen of England, has been hired to do the calligraphy work. It will be interesting to see how far the reconstruction goes, but any reconstruction of God's Word in Scripture must certainly fall into the camp of the historical-critical method.

On-going attempts by scholars in love with the historical-critical method seem to prevail in our day. They deceive and confuse. Any interpretation that falls short of honoring Scripture as the inerrant and infallible Word of God, is a hermeneutics *out of alinement*. It may be out of line with a contemporary, post-modern culture, but it certainly is not out of line with God and the authority of His Word. The question of authority still remains the central issue, as it was in Genesis 3. Whose voice is to be listened to today . . . God or man?

Authority over Scripture has not been the assumed, sole prerogative of scholars who openly sanction using the historical-critical method. It has also been appropriated by cult leaders and cult religions who deceive by preaching and teaching agreement with some parts of Scripture, only to add their own extra biblical spin as having more authority and truth than the Scriptures. To deny that the license taken by those committed to the historical-critical method has had any affect upon cult religions would be ridiculous. Once the lid of scriptural authority was pried loose after the Enlightenment and man's theories attempted to trump the authority of God's Word in Scripture, God's Word was questioned, trampled, ignored, and defiled. Man, God's highest creation of love, has been the victim ever since.

No one has to be convinced of the confusion and deception that runs rampant in our world today. It is everywhere. Are you tired of the many ways it has impacted upon your life? If so, you do not have to live as *a victim* of confusion and deception. God has a love message for you in His Son, Jesus, a love message in all of Holy Scripture that is in the *alinement of eternity*. It is in proper alinement by the same power of God Who created this world, Who sent His Son in our flesh, and Who, in Resurrection power, raised His Son from death, took Jesus in Ascended glory to His right hand, and as the Risen and Ascended Lord, now lives and reigns to all eternity as Lord, co-equal with the Father and the Holy Spirit, One God.

The proclamation of this is always before us in God's Word, the Holy Scriptures. Instead of allowing man the honor and the blessing of interpreting God's Word, wouldn't it be fitting and proper to allow God's Word to bring its own interpretation to man? This would be allowing God to make the connection of His Word with your life. If Holy Scripture is the Word of God, then this was and is, I believe, His intent and purpose when He inspired the first word to be written in the Holy Scriptures, all by the power of His Holy Spirit.

In the next chapter is my submission to you concerning what I believe to be God's way of making the connection between your life and His inerrant and infallible Word. It is the way of blessing and honor. It is the way of God's power, the Holy Spirit, for your life.

Notes

1. Darrell Jodock, op. cit. 5.
2. Ibid. 12.
3. Ibid. 102–103.
4. Ibid. 71.
5. Edgar V. McKnight, *Post-Modern Use of the Bible,* (Nashville: Abingdon Press, 1988).
6. Rudolph B. Skogerboe, *Who Has Stolen My Church?* (Grand Forks: Mike Beard and Associates, 1987), 100.
7. Darrell Jodock, op. cit. 87.
8. Jonah Blank, "*A Medieval Bible forModernTimes*",in *U.S.News & World Report*, 29 March 1999, 67.

Chapter 17

The Connection—
Scripture Is the Word of God!

All Scripture is inspired by God and profitable for teaching, for reproof, for correction, for training in righteousness; that the man of God may be adequate, equipped for every good work. (2 Tim. 3: 16, 17)

When Paul wrote the text quoted above in his second letter to Timothy, he wasn't writing from a position of his own authority. His authority came from God. It was God's Word that was written, not Paul's. That is the way it is with all of Scripture. There is one author Who has inspired the sixty-six books of the Bible. The connection of God with His Word is inseparable. This is such an obvious statement that it appears redundant, superfluous, repetitious. Yet, this obvious truth is the favorite target of man's scholarly assault on Scripture.

It is Johann Salomo Semler's scholarly descendants who "man the assault" and who join him in maintaining that not all of Scripture is the Word of God. Therefore, in trying to define what part of Scripture is the Word of God, liberal scholars have dumped confusion and deception on you and all of God's beloved. What they resist, with all the passion of their enlightened scholarship, is attributing all of Scripture to God as His inerrant and infallible Word. Instead, they attempt to add their spin, to stand as the interpreters of God's Word, while they leave the God Who inspired His Word in the shadows of obscurity. God isn't allowed to bring His interpretation, which is fully encased in His Word, to His beloved. The message and the Messenger have been attacked.

"God, as the interpreter of His Word?"—does this sound strange? To scholars in love with the historical-critical method, who don't want to allow God to be God, who don't want to yield to God's truth in Scripture, it certainly is. But to the child of God who longs and thirsts for God's truth, it is not strange at all. What is strange is the way life is interpreted today wherein we find ourselves in a culture that has elevated the individual to the autonomy of deity. Certainly, this has been our corporate reality since Genesis 3, but today, any suggestion that God has an authoritative Word, inerrant and infallible, is shunned as unacceptable by liberal biblical scholars. Absolutes are out and possibilities reign supreme in a culture which worships its belly button more than its Creator.

God, as the interpreter of His Word, is the Truth which makes the Bible come alive, because God's Spirit is the power through Whom the Bible is opened to you and to me. The Holy Spirit, in and through the Scriptures, creates faith, a gift of God. This is the causative authority of Scripture, which was discussed in Chapter 15 along with the normative authority. You will recall that the normative authority is the absolute authority of Scripture by which it is the norm and rule of faith. Simply put, it is the arbiter between what is true and what is false. It recognizes God's authority and not the "subjective experience" of theologians. As such, it provides the absolute standard, which God has established for the proclamation, the witness of the Good News in Jesus Christ as Lord and Savior. The causative authority is seen in Paul's first letter to the Corinthians, Chapter 12, verse 3: ". . . and no one can say 'Jesus is Lord,' except by the Holy Spirit."

The normative authority is seen in Jesus' words in John's Gospel, chapter 5, verse 39: "You search the Scriptures because you think that in them you have eternal life; and it is these that bear witness of me." These authorities are encased in all of Scripture and can not be separated from the holiness of God, His very being, as He has expressed it in His Word. (For more on the holiness of God, please refer to Leviticus 1:44–45; Leviticus 19:2; 1 Samuel 2:2; Psalm 60:6; Isaiah 6:3; 1 Peter 1:14–16; and Revelation 4:8.)

The power of interpretation resides in God, Himself. Therefore, since Scripture is God's Word, we must allow Scripture to interpret itself. This is no mystery at all. It simply means that Scripture has a clarity and unity whereby less clear passages in Scripture can be considered and understood in light of clear passages on the same subject. Regarding Scripture interpreting Scripture, Martin Luther wrote:

> I cannot bear it that they thus revile and blaspheme Scripture and the fathers. They accuse the Bible of being obscure, whereas all the fathers concede that it is the brightest light and take their own from it as David says (Ps. 119: 105): "Thy Word is my light." But they ascribe to the fathers the light with which they illuminate Scripture, whereas all the fathers concede their own obscurity and illuminate Scripture by Scripture alone. And, indeed, that is the right method. Scripture should be placed alongside Scripture in a right and proper way.

> He who can do this best is the best of the fathers. And all the books of the fathers we must read with discretion; they should not be taken on faith. But see whether they quote clear texts and explain Scripture by other clearer texts.[1]

Not only must Scripture interpret Scripture, but it must also be the anchor for sound doctrine.

In this sense, it stands as the rule of faith. Here faith is understood as doctrinal proclamations that are in accord and harmony with the teachings of Scripture. This is the foundation for the Lutheran Confessions. As true expositions of Scripture, they represent the faith of the Lutheran Church in terms of its doctrinal stance. Therefore, the Scriptures do not contradict themselves. If they did, there would be a shifting sand base for doctrine. Man would then be the supreme definer, and God, an addendum of malleable putty. God would be an impotent deity with little to say. Any trace of Law and Gospel would be non-existent. Spiritual chaos and death would reign supreme. Does this sound familiar?

The entire revelation of Scripture rises up as God's Word of Law and Gospel, to the chaotic, rebellious, sinful nature of man to which Genesis 3 attests. At the center of His Word is His Son, Jesus. Jesus overcomes for you and me what the Law condemns, our sinfulness. Central and foremost in Scripture is the presentation of Jesus as Savior of the world. Without the Law, we wouldn't know the curse of sin and the spiritual death that sin imparts. We would be hopeless animals playing King of the Mountain, worshipping at the shrines of our belly buttons. Thankfully, we do not have to live like that. God has a different script for us. He wrote that script in His Word to show our depravity in sin as we, and those before us, rebelled against Him as Lord. He wrote that script as our loving God Who did not abandon us, but sent His Son as Savior for sinners like us. Because of God's love for us, we have a Savior, Christ the Lord. This is Gospel, the good news of God in His Son for our salvation! The power of the Gospel is in the power of the Scriptures!

From Genesis to Revelation, the Scriptures hold together in the unity and clarity of God's love for us. Even the Law reveals God's love as His discipline for His beloved. The Gospel reveals God's love, which goes to the Cross of Calvary for you and for me. Scripture is God's love message in Jesus. There can be no more succinct definition of Scripture than that. Martin Luther, who stands among the centuries as God's man in love with God's Word, directed God's people to look for Christ in the Bible. In an explanation he gave concerning Psalm 40, he wrote,

> Let the Holy Spirit Himself read this Book to His own if He desires to be understood. For it does not write about men or about making a living (*vom Bauch*), as all the other books do, but about the fact that God's Son was obedient to His Father for us and fulfilled His will. Whoever does not need this wisdom should let this Book lie; it does not benefit them anyway. It teaches another and eternal life, of which reason knows nothing and is able to comprehend nothing. Let him, then, who would study in this Book make up his mind to look for nothing in it except that of which the psalm speaks: that the Son of God willingly and obediently became a burnt offering for us in order to appease God's wrath.[2]

Another important consideration that opens Scripture as the Word of God to you, God's beloved, is to understand that when the Holy Spirit inspired the Scriptures to be written, He inspired them to be written in human language. He did not write them in code. He did not write them for the highly educated. He wrote them in the clarity of the language of man so that the most humble in mind among us can understand the message. In a sermon I preached at St. John's, Hatboro, Pennsylvania, in 1961, I said: "The Gospel can be understood by the most intelligent minds as well as by the simple minded." Or at least that's what I meant and thought I said! My congregation, upon leaving church that Sunday, told me that I concluded that sentence of the sermon with these words: "The Gospel can be understood by you, the simple minded." In good nature and in jest, they identified themselves to me as they left church "as the simple minded of St. John's." To this day, I am still reminded of their impression of what they "thought" they heard me say. Can one voice dispute the ears of hundreds?

The importance of understanding the message is essential. God, in His love, would have it no other way. Therefore, when interpreting the words and sentences of Scripture, the grammatical usage of language conveys the message and must be observed. The word *grammatical*, as used here, means the "laws of language," the instrument through which the understanding of the words can be comprehended. Before any theological connection can be made, the message must first be understood. The meaning of words is the essence of communication. That is why a reliable dictionary of the Bible and a commentary that is in harmony with Scripture as the Word of God are indispensable tools for the lay person as you read the Word of God.

In no way does this mean a surrender to the historical-critical method. This is because you are not standing as a judge over the Word of God, but are standing as one seeking the grammatical understanding of the words of Scripture, not seeking to reject or call into question the Word of God. When the words are understood, as their understanding comes by the power of the Holy Spirit, the message of God in Christ for our salvation radiates with the clarity and brilliance of the sun that God created. Yes, we can literally read the Holy Scriptures as God's truth, His love message in Jesus for our salvation, because in the faith our God supplies, we believe Jesus is our Lord and Savior. Again, Martin Luther adds illumination to this truth.

> No violence should be done the Words of God, neither by a man nor by an angel; but as far as possible we should retain them in their simplest meaning and take them in their grammatical and literal sense, unless an obvious circumstance plainly forbids it, lest we give our adversaries occasion to make a mockery of all Scripture.[3]

The clarity and simplicity of God's Word in Scripture, all by the power of the Holy Spirit, must not be thrown into confusion and deception by human authorities who, by their enlightened authority (by virtue of the historical-critical method), attempt to have the final word regarding God's Word. God's people do not need that type of "spin." Again, a love story does not have to be made into a mystery.

The connection of Scripture as the Word of God to the child of God must always be one of submission wherein the person addressed by that Word believes that God is speaking in and through His Word. It is the created, standing in fear and awe of his or her Creator. In order to understand the meaning of that fear, Luther has given a lucid explanation.

> Being afraid of God is different from fearing God. The fear of God is a fruit of love, but being afraid of Him is the seed of hatred. Therefore we should not be afraid of God but should fear Him so that we do not hate Him whom we should love. . . . Therefore the fear of God is more aptly called reverence. For example, we revere those whom we love, honor, esteem, and fear to offend.[4]

The right connection to the Word of God is being in the proper alinement with that Word as God has willed and has revealed. It is as Kurt Marquart so aptly put it: "Giving God 'the honor of truthfulness.'" Marquart pointed out that giving God the honor of truthfulness is at the heart of inerrancy, and that without the giving of that honor, the principle of *sola Scriptura,* by Scripture alone, becomes an empty pretense.[5]

The truthfulness of God's Word is the warp and woof of the texture of Scripture. What you and I read in God's Word is a message like no other message we have ever encountered. It is an empowered message of God wherein the Holy Spirit can make the words come alive in our lives. Because it is God speaking to us in words that are continually fresh and new, there can never be a time when they dry up as parched words because of repetition.

I have yet to meet a biblical scholar who can say that he or she has exhausted the outpouring of the Holy Spirit in Scripture. Our God keeps making endless connections of His truth of Law and Gospel as that truth centers upon His Son, Jesus, for our salvation. The Word of God never changes. The Word of God has endless power to lead us into heights of truth, the truth that coincides with all of Scripture. The more you and I are connected to God and His Word, the more wonder and praise for our God of truth emanates from our thankful hearts. We see truth as we never saw it before, because we are led by God's Holy Spirit to see the truth of Jesus in the full power of God's Word.

When you and I have the Bible in hand and read it as God's inerrant and infallible Word, we are blessed as we honor His Word. In no way do we worship the Bible, so as to be accused of biblicism. We worship our God: Father, Son, and Holy Spirit. We worship Him because He has shown His love to us and has brought us into new life through His Son, Jesus. This is the Good News that God pours upon lives who are open to Him through the power of the Holy Spirit in His Word in Scripture. God, Himself, interprets Scripture for us. Scripture is the inerrant and infallible Word of God. Our Holy God has spoken!

Martin Luther had it right when he wrote:

> They (the Jews, John 8:25) desire to know who He is and not to regard what He says, while He desires them first to listen; then they will know who He is. The rule is: Listen and allow the Word to make the beginning, then the knowing will nicely follow. If, however, you do not listen, you will never know anything. For it is decreed: God will not be seen, known, or comprehended except through His Word alone. Whatever, therefore, one undertakes for salvation apart from the Word is in vain. God will not respond to that. He will not have it. He will not tolerate any other way. Therefore, let His Book, in which He speaks with you, be commended to you; for He did not cause it to be written for no purpose. He did not want us to let it lie there in neglect, as if He were speaking with mice under the bench or with flies on the pulpit. We are to read it, to think and speak about it, and to study it, certain that He Himself (not an angel or a creature) is speaking with us in it.[6]

Another quote is in order, a quote from seventy plus years ago. It still resonates the timeless position of the LCMS wherein Scripture is the Word of God. This, I hope you have seen in this work as a stark contrast against the "enlightened" scholarship of sinful man, with their biblical spin, which holds God's Word in question and judgment.

> The Lutheran Church differs from all other churches in being essentially the Church of the pure Word and unadulterated Sacraments. Not with the great number of

> her adherents, not her organizations, not her charitable and other institutions, not her beautiful customs and liturgical forms, etc., but the precious truths confessed by her symbols in perfect agreement with the Holy Scriptures constitute the true beauty and rich treasure of our Church, as well as the never-failing source of her vitality and power.[7]

When Scripture is held as God's inerrant and infallible Word, be assured that God will bless His Word to you and that He will honor what He blesses. With our God, it can be no other way!

Soli Deo Gloria!

Notes

1. Martin Luther, *What Luther Says,* op. cit., vol. I, 88, #268.
2. Ibid., vol. I, 81, #248.
3. Ibid., vol. I, 92, #283.
4. Ibid., vol. I, 509, #1525.
5. Kurt Marquart, in *Studies in Lutheran Hermeneutics,* eds. John Reumann, Samuel H. Nafzger, and Harold H. Ditmanson, (Philadelphia: Fortress Press, 1979), 321.
6. Martin Luther, *What Luther Says,* op. cit., vol. I, 81, #246.
7. *Concordia Triglotta,* ed. F. Bente, (St. Louis: Concordia Publishing House, 1921), iv.

To order more copies of

BLESSING & HONOR HONOR & BLESSING

Understanding The Confusion/Deception of Biblical Spin

send $14.99 plus $3.95 shipping and handling to

BOOKS ETC.
P.O. Box 4888
Seattle, WA 98104

or have your credit card ready and call:

(800) 917 – BOOK